Other titles of interest

ADVANCES IN BEHAVIOUR RESEARCH AND THERAPY
A Journal for Reviews and Reports of Original Research
Editors: H. J. EYSENCK and S. RACHMAN, Institute of Psychiatry, London.

This new review journal encourages and facilitates the dissemination of new ideas, findings and formulations in the field of behaviour modification and therapy. It provides research and clinical workers with the opportunity to describe progress and convey their ideas in depth.

Four issues per year

Concept Formation

by

NEIL BOLTON

PERGAMON PRESS

OXFORD · NEW YORK · SYDNEY · TORONTO
PARIS · FRANKFURT

U. K.	Pergamon Press Ltd., Headington Hill Hall, Oxford OX3 0BW, England
U. S. A.	Pergamon Press Inc., Maxwell House, Fairview Park, Elmsford, New York 10523, U.S.A.
C A N A D A	Pergamon of Canada Ltd., 75 The East Mall, Toronto, Ontario, Canada
A U S T R A L I A	Pergamon Press (Aust.) Pty. Ltd., 19a Boundary Street, Rushcutters Bay, N.S.W. 2011, Australia
F R A N C E	Pergamon Press SARL, 24 rue des Ecoles, 75240 Paris, Cedex 05, France
WEST GERMANY	Pergamon Press GmbH, 6242 Kronberg-Taunus, Pferdstrasse 1, West Germany

First edition 1977

Library of Congress Cataloging in Publication Data

Bolton, Neil.

Concept formation.

Includes bibliographical references and index.
1. College students — Psychology. 2. Concepts
I. Title
LB3609.B65 1977   153.2'3   76—58836
ISBN 0—08—021493—2 (Hardcover)
ISBN 0—08—021494—0 (Flexicover)

Printed in Great Britain by Page Bros (Norwich) Ltd.

To Suzanne

Contents

List of Figures

CHAPTER 1

Introduction

What is the meaning of the term "concept"? Since we employ concepts to refer to a variety of experiences, for instance, to experiences of physical objects and relationships and to experiences of personal qualities and social relationships, are there different psychological processes corresponding to these different "types" of concept? Do children form concepts in the same way that adults form them? How important is language in concept formation? Are there individual differences in concept formation and what are the best ways in which people can be instructed to extend and refine their conceptual systems? And, finally, can we advance to a psychological theory of concept formation which is comprehensive enough to provide answers to questions as diverse as the above? These are some of the questions that are of particular importance in the light of what is currently known. It is hoped that the present account will provide some help towards answering them, but, before we begin, it may be as well to state some of the assumptions which have guided me.

There are two major and apparently conflicting theories of the nature of concept formation. The traditional theory, known as the theory of abstraction or as the "copy theory", is that concepts are formed by the subject abstracting (i.e. "drawing away") certain resemblances among otherwise dissimilar stimuli. On this view, a concept is a representation of the generalities we have observed to occur among our many particular perceptions. The opposing point of view is that a concept is formed, not by the subject merely attending to such general features, but by his having a particular hypothesis about certain features of his environment. Because he has a hypothesis, the subject can search for evidence which supports or invalidates it. In the course of development subjects come to organize their hypotheses to form conceptual systems and in this sense it can be said that the person constructs his view of the world. It is easy to see that these opposing views correspond to the distinction between induction and deduction: in inductive reasoning progress is from the particular to the general, whereas in deductive reasoning particular truths are attained through the use of general hypotheses.

It has been argued that a choice does not have to be made between these two alternatives, for a complete theory of how concepts are formed would be one which allowed the subject both to group elements by observed resemblances and to see connections through the use of hypotheses. Vinacke (1952) reasoned that abstraction and hypothesis-testing should not be regarded as mutually exclusive activities, since either or both may occur, depending upon the conditions and the individual.

> "Under some conditions, the individual may be essentially a passive recipient of sensory impressions which gradually summate into the concept. Under other conditions, it may be that an individual proceeds by establishing a hypothesis and then deliberately checking it against instances" (p. 107).

This conclusion, Vinacke believed, is especially warranted with respect to concept formation in adults, although it may be that in relation to concept formation in children the theory of abstraction is the most relevant.

Such a solution appears reasonable, but I believe that it is not. It is no doubt true that sometimes we have a fairly definite idea or hypothesis of what we are looking for and that on other occasions we have to examine the problem-material without benefit of such explicit guidance. But it is surely false to conclude from this that the organism is on some occasions a passive recipient of sensations and that there are two different types of process in concept formation. For the basic fault with this suggested reconciliation of the two points of view is that it perpetuates the division between sensory experience on the one hand and ideas and hypotheses on the other, between what is imposed upon the organism by its environment and what the organism imposes upon the environment, and it becomes impossible to describe how these two interact in a reciprocal manner. Thus, concepts are formed through the subject's experiences of particular instances, as the theory of abstraction holds, but these instances do not impose themselves on a passive organism with no point of view of its own; similarly, a concept can always be regarded as the expression of a hypothesis about a particular aspect of reality, but this hypothesis is not formed prior to experience. Whatever differences exist between inductive and deductive accounts of concept formation, they share the more fundamental error of assuming that reality is already defined for the subject, that is, that the elements which make up a concept-to-be-learned are "there" for the subject whose only task consists either of attending to them or of interpreting them with the aid of a well-formed hypothesis. But these no longer sound adequate accounts of concept formation. It now seems much more likely that the subject elaborates his repertoire of concepts at the same time that he organizes his environment and, consequently, we should speak of the construction of reality occurring in parallel with the development of cognitive structures such as hypotheses, concepts and plans.

It may be that the persistence of the theory of abstraction has been in part due to the opposing use of terms such as hypothesis or plan, which suggest an ability that is mature and conscious. We surely do not go about our ordinary lives armed with hypotheses in the manner of a scientist performing a well-controlled experiment. Nevertheless, this usage ought not to obscure the insight central to this school of thought that behaviour is never a mere reaction to stimuli but is always guided by an aim, however dimly defined this is for the subject or the observer. One way of expressing this state of affairs is to say that consciousness is always intentional. A concept cannot be a particular copy of a reality which exists independently of the subject's activities, because it is formed through those activities and these activities are the expression of the subject's search for meaning. The idea that experience is intentional is implicit in all those psychological theories which deserve to be called "cognitive". It is to be found in Miller, Galanter and Pribram's (1960) notion of *plans* that guide behaviour, in Bartlett's (1932) use of the concept of *schema* to denote the reconstructive rather than the reproductive nature of remembering, in Kelly's (1955) ideas about the *constructs* which people employ to predict events and make sense of reality, and in Piaget's theory (Piaget, 1950) that the child develops a system of *schemes* from the co-ordination of his actions upon objects.

However, whilst there has been a growing readiness among psychologists to accept the thesis that experience and behaviour are guided by cognitive structures, criticisms of the traditional theory of abstraction have come from philosophers more than psychologists. But psychologists have tended to study concept formation without reference to philosophical problems of truth and knowledge. It could be argued that this strategy is admissible in so far as we can distinguish the psychological problem of describing concept learning from the philosophical problem of describing the conditions under which we can be said to know something; on this reasoning, psychologists are interested in accounting for thinking, philosophers in accounting for our knowledge of reality. Now, convenient though this separation appears to be, it has two major, undesirable consequences. In the first place, the avoidance of philosophical speculation by psychologists has meant that they have tended to accept without question the notion of the traditional theory of abstraction that concept formation is to do with classification; consequently, they have ignored the many other ways in which subjects organize experience. I hope to show that speculation on the nature of concepts forces us to recognize the special place of class concepts within a broader framework and I shall argue that we must define what a concept is in the most general terms in order to account for the existence of various modes of thinking. But, secondly, the subject of concept formation has suffered because the avoidance of discussion about questions of truth and error has debased the very notion of thinking itself. For the aim of thinking is knowing. We think in order to know. Thus, it is logically impossible to devise an adequate psychological theory of thinking without explaining how thinking fulfils or fails to fulfil its aim. Frege (1918) identified the crucial issue when he asserted that a thought or concept is something for which the question of truth arises. The explanation of concept formation is, then, necessarily involved in a wider and more profound study of knowledge and must account for the logical nature of concepts and their reference to reality.

If it is true that, with the notable exception of Piaget, psychologists have failed to do justice to the complexities of concept formation, since they have relied implicitly upon too narrow a theoretical framework, then it follows that we must resort to reflection upon our experience in order to determine how many different sorts of concepts there are, the manner in which they function, and the way in which they enable us to understand reality. I believe that psychologists are inclined to dismiss too readily the work of those who relied upon analysis of experience and reflection on the grounds that they carried out no experiments. This should not need saying but, in the present climate of opinion, it does: there are many insights to be gained through intelligent reflection upon experience, and methodological rigour will not save one's research from triviality or error if we have failed in the first place to define properly our concepts and area of study.

These are some of the assumptions which have guided this account of concept formation. It is assumed, first, that concepts are formed, not simply inductively, that is, through observation of environmental regularities, nor simply deductively, through the application of already-formed cognitive structures to events and objects, but through the reciprocal interaction of cognitive structures and environmental events. We develop concepts through testing them against reality and we develop a knowledge of the world through the elaboration of concepts and conceptual systems. It is assumed, secondly, that the psychology of concept formation is necessarily involved in questions about the nature of that reality, since we think in order to know, and, thirdly, that the exploration of concept formation can profit from both the application of experimental methods and the analysis of experience.

The chapters that follow are written on the basis of these assumptions. Part I is concerned with the theoretical and philosophical basis for the study of concept formation; Chapter 2 criticizes the traditional theory of concept formation and suggests certain requirements for a comprehensive theory; Chapter 3 looks at the phenomenology of concept learning; and Chapter 4 is a brief account of the possibility of the existence of various types of concept and conceptual system. Part II is directed at empirical studies of concept formation; Chapter 5 looking at preconceptual developments; Chapter 6 at the growth of concepts from childhood to adolescence; Chapter 7 at the problem of the mechanisms responsible for the child learning concepts; Chapter 8 at some of the experimental work on concept attainment in adults; and Chapter 9 at the question of individual differences in concept learning. Finally, Part III inquires into the possible implications of the work reviewed in the first two sections of the book; Chapter 10 considers the educational implications and Chapter 11 briefly summarizes the major theoretical implications.

PART I

THEORETICAL BASES OF CONCEPT FORMATION

CHAPTER 2

Towards a Theory of Concept Formation

There is no one satisfactory theory of concept formation. On the one hand, the traditional theory — the theory of abstraction — has been shown to be inadequate by a number of authors (for example, Husserl, 1900; Cassirer, 1923; Geach, 1957; Arnheim, 1970), but psychological research is not sufficiently advanced to permit a systematic statement of an alternative viewpoint. Subsequent chapters will review and discuss this research in order to assess the progress that has been made towards a valid theory of concept formation, but we must begin by considering the deficiencies of the traditional theory in order to understand as clearly as possible the underlying theoretical issues.

The theory of abstraction, which can be traced back to Aristotle and through the British empiricist philosophers, notably Locke (1690) and Hume (1739), states that concepts are formed through a process in which the person recognizes similarities or identical elements in a set of objects; he thus abstracts these resemblances away from the other properties of the set of objects that are not relevant to the concept. Thus, the concept of "man" is formed by noting the features which all men have in common and by ignoring differences in, say, height or colour. Of course, elementary concepts can be combined to form more complex classifications and a favourite pastime of psychologists interested in concept learning is to ask subjects to acquire such concepts, for example, as "all cards with red diamonds in the centre". But for the theory of abstraction there is no fundamental difference between the formation of simple concepts and the formation of complex concepts. The child first learns simple, concrete concepts, such as "mummy" or "table", and later learns more abstract concepts like "addition" or "religion". Concrete concepts, it is maintained, are the first to be learned, because we abstract from experience

9

of things and make generalizations from our experience of particular things.

There are, perhaps, three major assumptions inherent in this theory of concept formation. The first is that concepts are formed through people recognizing resemblances among stimuli. Note that it is assumed that the resemblances are a property of the subject's environment and that his task is to attend to them. We may say, then, that when a subject has formed a concept he has formed a copy of reality, or one aspect of it, and the more advanced he is in conceptual development, the better his copy will be. The second assumption is that progress in concept formation is from the particular to the general: the subject first observes particular events and then, noting the resemblances between some of them, develops the generalization which enables him to group these particular events as instances of a class. Thus, the child's perception of particular triangles leads to the general concept of a triangle. The third assumption is that concrete concepts are primary in the sense that they lay the foundation for the development of abstract concepts, including logical and mathematical concepts, which are assumed to be concerned with relationships between things. On this view, logico-mathematical knowledge is derived from physical knowledge — our experience of the physical world — since logical and mathematical rules are reflections of the workings of this world. It follows that in a different physical environment there would be logical and mathematical rules other than those to which we are accustomed.

Each of these three basic assumptions has been challenged. In considering the criticisms that have been levelled against the traditional theory of abstraction we shall see that each of these assumptions is highly implausible and that an alternative, psychologically plausible view emerges that is opposed to the traditional one on all three counts.

Recognition and Intention

The objections to the abstractionist principle that we form simple concepts by recognizing resemblances among otherwise dissimilar stimuli may be summarized briefly. Geach (1957) takes as an example of a simple concept the idea of "chromatic colour", which he holds to be no less simple, in the sense that it is, as the abstractionist puts it, "given in direct perception", than the concept of "red". Geach argues:

"Now it is quite impossible that I should form this concept, 'chromatic colour', by discriminative attention to a feature given in my visual experience. In looking at a red window-pane I have not two sensations, one of redness and one barely of chromatic colour; there are not, for that matter, two distinct sense-given features, one of them making my sensation to be barely a sensation of chromatic colour, the other making it a sensation of redness. If I abstract from what differentiates red from other chromatic colours, I am abstracting from red itself; red is not a chromatic colour *plus a differentia*, so that we can concentrate our attention upon chromatic colour and abstract from the *differentia*" (p. 37).

It is clear that our perception of the red window-pane does not contain two distinct features corresponding to the concepts, "red" and "chromatic colour". What can be said, however, is that the perceiver himself may employ two or more concepts to refer to the same object. The idea that the act of recognition is the necessary foundation for concept formation is mistaken since, as Cassirer (1953) has pointed out also, the same elements can be organized in many different ways according to the point of view which the person adopts. And to adopt a point of view is to employ some principle by which the elements are grouped together to form a concept. But the theory of abstraction is silent over this quite crucial characteristic of the concept. It has no means of accounting for the development of different rules of relation. The reason for this omission is not difficult to discern: it is because for this theory the subject's only activity consists of attending to and grouping sensations that are "given" to him. Here we have a one-way causality — the world impresses itself upon a subject who has no point of view of his own — and it becomes quite impossible to do justice to the diversity of points of view which inform our concepts.

However, there is a way in which the traditional theory that concepts are formed through abstraction of resemblances may be saved. Wittgenstein (1953), as is well known, pointed out that there is no common element to be found in concepts such as "games" or "tools" or "beauty". "Think of the tools in a tool-box: there is a hammer, pliers, a saw, a screwdriver, a rule, a gluepot, glue, nails, and screws — the functions of words are as diverse as the functions of these objects." He suggested that what makes us use the same word for all examples is that they are related to one another in many different ways in "a complicated network of similarities overlapping and criss-crossing". He called these similarities "family resemblances", for the various resemblances between members of a family overlap and criss-cross in the same way. Wittgenstein's views appear to offer a way out for a theory of concept formation which aims to derive the concept from attention to stimulus properties alone: instead of a class with a common element, we have a loosely related cluster or "complex" (Vygotsky, 1962).

But one can argue that this is not the case (Mandelbaum, 1965). Wittgenstein failed to make explicit that when one refers to *family* resemblances, there exists a genetic connection between individuals as well as physical resemblances. If, observing a number of photographs, we were able to point to certain resemblances among the people portrayed, we would speak of resemblances, and not a family resemblance. Members of a family are related through a common ancestry. Such a relationship is not itself one of the specific perceptual features of those who share a family resemblance; none the less, it is crucial in differentiating them from those who are not to be regarded as members of a single family. Similarly, in the case of "games" or "art" the analogue to genetic ties might be the purpose for the sake of which various games were invented or the intentions behind works of art (wish-fulfilment or presentation of truth in sensuous form). It is only by recourse to purpose and motives, in short, to intentionality, that we are led not to link solitaire to fortune-telling or wrestling to fighting, in spite of there being many points of resemblance.

In order to understand the development of concepts, therefore, it is necessary to start from an alternative conception of the relationship between perceiver and perceived, one which insists upon the subject playing an active role in interpreting and structuring reality. This means, at one level of explanation, opposing to the traditional view of consciousness formulated by the empiricist philosophers, who regarded consciousness as "nothing but a bundle of different perceptions which succeed each other with an inconceivable rapidity" (Hume, 1739, p. 252), the doctrine of the "intentionality of consciousness", formulated among others by Husserl (1901, 1929) and the phenomenologists. This doctrine states that consciousness is always consciousness of something – I perceive a tree, am afraid of spiders, laugh at a joke. Thus, in every act of perception or thinking there is, on the one hand, the psychological act (thinking, laughing, etc.) and, on the other hand, the object of this act. If you are looking at a painting, for example, the painting appears at a certain distance, involves a certain content, arouses interest, and so forth. Husserl called this the *noema* of perception: it is the object such as the perceiving subject is aware of it and intends it. The noema is distinguished from the act itself, which is called the *noesis*, and from the real object. The painting, as a real object, appears now in this particular manner, but on subsequent occasions may be perceived quite differently. Consequently, although the real object can only be experienced as such through a series of perceptions, it must not be confused with a single *noema*. But now we come to a fundamental point. If I stand and look at the painting, it may be said that my conscious experience consists of a number of perceptual acts, which are all different from one another. Yet, although the acts differ, I experience the same object: the painting presents itself now exactly as it did a moment ago or as it will do tomorrow. We have, then, the experience of being confronted with an identical object, but this experience would be impossible if consciousness consisted, as Hume argued, merely of sensations succeeding one another. As Gurwitsch (1964) points out, the traditional conception of consciousness, in which emphasis is placed upon temporality — the succession of acts and their dispersion over time — is incomplete, for no mental state is to be conceived only and exclusively as a temporal event in the stream of consciousness. The sense of identity is a fact of consciousness, no less authentic and fundamental than temporality. We shall see in subsequent chapters that psychologists concerned with conceptual development have recognized the importance of this sense of identity.

To say that consciousness is intentional is to say that it is to be defined by its reference to a sense or meaning. Intentionality refers to the objectivating function of consciousness. This function consists of confronting the subject with meanings which retain their identity through successive acts. There are perceptual meanings, conceptual meanings, syntactical meanings, and so forth, corresponding to different spheres of reality. But in each case the consequence of this analysis is a rejection of the assumption that sensory impressions are "given" to the subject. This implication was clearly recognized by Dewey (1930) when he wrote that "the history of the theory of knowledge would have been different if, instead of the word 'data' or 'givens', it had happened to start with calling the qualities in question 'takens'" (pp. 170–1). Dewey's (1896) earlier critique of the reflex-arc concept led him to propose a functionalist usage of the terms,

stimulus and response, in which these are viewed, not as independent elements, but as different aspects of a sensori-motor co-ordination; thus, a
motor response (attending, moving towards, etc.) determines the stimulus
and the response is an attempt to bring about a change in the stimulus.
For example, there is not first a sound and then the activity of attention,
because it is the motor response which constitutes that which becomes the
stimulus to, say, flight. And flight is not merely a motor activity, for it
has a sensory value and is engaged in so that this stimulus value might be
changed. Miller, Galanter and Pribram (1960) have argued that Dewey's
"circuit", which matches the concept of the feedback-loop in cybernetics,
is the basic unit of behaviour.

The Particular and the General

The word "abstract" means literally "to draw away from". The theory
of abstraction states that a concept is a generalization "drawn away" from
a number of particular impressions and that it thereby represents the
resemblances which exist among the particulars. Now, Husserl (1900, 1901)
and, later, Schutz (1966) have argued that this doctrine confuses two
meanings of the term abstract, which ought to be clearly distinguished. On
the one hand, it is true that certain particular types can be subsumed
under a general category (as when we ignore the differences between
spaniels, fox-terriers and poodles and call them "dogs"), but it would be
wrong to conclude that this form of behaviour is representative of the
psychological process of concept formation. Indeed, to be able to subsume certain particulars under a general category requires that the general
concept has already been acquired, for, if this were not the case, we would
not be able to generalize from one to the other. We would not be able to
group spaniels along with fox-terriers unless the quality of "doginess" had
already been grasped in the one and extended to the other. Thus, whilst
"dog" as an abstract concept may be defined by reference to the resemblances among the particular types, the concept of dog is not formed
through a noting of the resemblances among the particular types, since
there must be some intuition of the general in the perception of the particular. It was to this act of intuition that Husserl (1901) gave the name of
"ideational abstraction" in order to distinguish it from the traditional and

mistaken view that abstraction is from the particular to the general. There is an interesting parallel between this distinction and that made by Bruner, Goodnow and Austin (1956) between concept formation and concept attainment. The latter refers to the activity of grouping elements into categories which are already clearly understood and defined (as, for instance, when an adult subject is asked to sort stimuli by colour and shape), but concept formation refers to the activity of forming and defining a concept. The distinction seems a useful one, although, as Pikas (1966) has pointed out, it may be somewhat difficult to determine in practice, since concepts must be formed through the subject encountering instances or they may begin a task by grouping elements according to a well-defined category but find in the course of this activity that the category itself changes or becomes clearer.

But what is meant by the intuition of the general in the particular must now be defined more precisely. To begin, note that there is no such experience as the experience of an isolated object: there is no particular percept. A perception which presents one aspect of an object to us is charged with potentialities which may be fulfilled as the object is explored. Phenomenologists employ the concept of *horizon* to denote the totality of organized potentialities involved in the perception of an object. Thus, my perception of this table on entering the room does not present me with an isolated object, because the object is perceived in the context of my past perceptions and my potential actions in exploring the object. Every object has an inner and an outer horizon. Exploration of the thing itself results in an extension of our understanding of it, but the object also has an outer horizon: this table exists beside an armchair, in a room of a certain shape, colour, and so forth. It is apparent, then, that with the notion of horizon there must of necessity be a reference to temporal succession, or, more precisely, to the unity of our successive experiences. This unity is possible because each object is experienced as a typical one. Having experience of other tables, I expect the present one to reveal those characteristics which typify a table when I come to explore the object in more detail. Schutz (1966) says that "what has been experienced in the actual perception of one object is apperceptively transferred to any other similar object, perceived merely as to its type" (pp. 281–2). Of course, further experience may or may not confirm the initial typification, so that new sub-categories may have to be established, because

the known type always contains a horizon of still unknown characteristics pertaining to particular examples of the type. These new categories
would, then, form sub-types. But the important point to note is that
the fundamental psychological process in concept formation is, not
the subsumption of particulars under a general category, but an act by
which a particular element comes to be regarded as an example of a
type. As this process is accomplished as a result of the subject's intentions and points of view, it follows that the concept is essentially predictive: to form a concept is to anticipate that certain future experiences
will take a certain form. The predictive nature of concepts has been
stressed by Kelly (1955). Personal Construct Theory is concerned mainly
with understanding the ways in which people construe each other, but
Kelly's notions about the nature of constructs may be equally applicable
to physical objects and events. In particular, the idea that constructs
are equivalent to the hypotheses of the scientist and that they are capable
of validation or invalidation parallel the views of Husserl and Schutz on
the nature of concepts. There is a further parallel, surely, with Bartlett's
(1932) notion of a 'schema' and Piaget's (1950) notion of a 'scheme'.
Bartlett defined a schema as "an active organisation of past reactions, or of
past experiences, which must always be supposed to be operating in any
well-adapted organic responses" (p. 201). Remembering is, therefore,
primarily a reconstructive, not a reproductive, process, since the subject
relates present events to established schemata: "In remembering, the subject
uses the setting, or scheme, or pattern, and builds up its characteristics afresh
to aid whatever response the needs of the moment may demand" (p. 208).

The generality of a concept is not, then, something which is acquired
in the final stage of concept formation, for generality is implicit in the
experience of what we call the particular. But there is another source
for the generality of the concept — the fact that the individual develops
in a society in which there are agreed names for objects and events. If
language did not possess the power of communicating agreed meaning,
then our concepts would remain idiosyncratic and incommunicable.
Concepts are the expression of shared meanings and, in this sense, they
are socially constructed. Social cooperation and conventions stabilize
concepts because an agreed name can be given to the same experience.
This does not mean that we should identify the formation of a concept
solely with the ability to give that concept a name; as we shall see, there

are other psychological processes besides language which are equally important. But it does mean that, in searching for the origins of concept formation, we must look to the child's acquisition of language as one important influence.

Logico-mathematical and Physical Experience

The final issue concerns the distinction between concepts of things and concepts of logical and mathematical relations. There appears to be a qualitative difference between these two types of concept. For example, the logical operations of "not", "if . . . then", and so forth, as well as the mathematical operators, do not refer to things which exist in the way that "dog" or "religion" do. How, then, can logical concepts be abstracted from our experience of the world, for there are no examples of "not-ness" to be inspected in things? Yet the traditional theory of abstraction offers us no alternative, since it affirms that all concepts are derived from our experience of the world — a view which led Mill (1874) to suppose that in a different world 5 + 4 might amount to 8, not 9. This viewpoint was criticized by Frege (1884) and Husserl (1900) who pointed out that, if logico-mathematical laws were derived from experience, then they could only be stated as probabilities; all we could say about 5 added to 4 would be that it is a matter of probability that they will amount to 9, since we might encounter conditions in which they produced a different total. But that this outcome does injustice to the nature of these laws is evident from the fact that their results are certain in so far as one correctly follows the rules of the system. It must be concluded, therefore, that the traditional theory of abstraction has no means of accounting for the development of these concepts.

This limitation stems from a restricted definition of the nature of experience, which is seen as always entailing an abstraction from things in the environment. However, once the intentional nature of conscious experience is grasped, the way is open for an analysis of the forms which this experience assumes. Husserl (1929) began this programme in *Experience and Judgement*, in which he argued that logical performance is evident at all levels of experience and knowledge, and not only on the relatively high levels of formal, linguistic statements with which logic traditionally starts.

He saw his task as that of clarifying the origin of logical performance in pre-predicative experience, that is, experience prior to the conscious distinction between subject and object. Consider, for example, the origin of the idea of negation. Instead of an intention being fulfilled, it may be disappointed. Thus, it may be found that the perceived red colour on a sphere is not spread over the whole object, which turns out to be green in part and not the anticipated red. There is here a conflict between the intention and the perception of the thing as it "really is" and the latter has a force and certainty which overwhelms the anticipation of the whole being red. By such descriptions of the origin of logical operators, Husserl aimed to show that they are not first of all a matter of predicative judgement but already occur in primitive form in pre-predicative experience.

It may be said that Piaget's guiding aim too is to determine the essential features of logico-mathematical experience, for, like Husserl, he holds that logical knowledge extends to the developmentally earliest experiences. In order to understand Piaget's thesis, it is necessary to begin with the distinction between physical experience and logico-mathematical experience. To illustrate this distinction, Piaget (in Beth and Piaget, 1966) gives the example of a child playing with a number of pebbles. The child can in the course of his explorations discover more about the properties of the pebbles, their weight, texture, and so forth: this knowledge can be called physical knowledge since the child has found out something about the pebbles themselves. But he may also discover, when he lays the pebbles in a row before him, that he arrives at the same total when he counts from right to left as when he counts from left to right. Now, this discovery is an example of logico-mathematical knowledge, since the child has found out something, not about the pebbles themselves, but about the consequences of his own actions and the ways in which they can be co-ordinated. In Piagetian theory, therefore, logical and mathematical operations are internalized systems of actions, and this kind of knowledge can be distinguished from physical knowledge. But, although they may be distinguished, so that we can say that the developing child learns more both about the nature of the world and the structure of his actions, these are necessarily interdependent developments, since to advance in understanding reality presupposes a system of interco-ordinated actions (the child would not understand the concept of weight properly unless he were able to understand the operations of relating elements in a series), and in order for these operational systems to develop, the child must have experience of physical reality. Piaget's developmental analysis consists, therefore, of tracing the emergence of these interdependent modes of knowledge from their origins in sensori-motor experience to their most advanced forms in logical and mathematical thinking. He uses the notion of adaptation to describe this process. Adaptation is said to involve assimilation, the relating of an object or event to an existing cognitive structure or *scheme*, and accommodation, the adjustment of schemes to the demands of objects and events.

In this way, we may attempt to reconcile a psychological explanation of the development of logical concepts with what we know about the nature of these concepts. Logical and mathematical concepts are necessary and possess universal validity because they express the essential structures of the actions and operations which we employ to make sense of the world. The actions which become internalized in systems of operations are, according to Piaget, those actions which are common to all men, for, despite variations in environments and cultural values, all our actions are developed and systematized in certain definite ways, and we may thus speak of the "epistemic subject", that is, the subject who is capable of understanding reality in a way that is universally valid, as well as the individual subject or the subject shaped by a particular culture.

But, although we may talk of the general features of conceptualization, those forces which constrain and channel the development of concepts into particular forms must not be ignored. The subject develops in a particular environment to which he must adapt in order to survive; he is a member of a certain society at a certain period in time; he uses a particular language and is guided by certain values. These facts raise the question of the extent to which concept formation is influenced by social and linguistic variations. Do people in different cultures have quite different concepts of reality according to their different preoccupations and habits? Or does the fact that logico-mathematical concepts derive from internalized and general actions ensure that this form of concept formation at least assumes a similar form and runs a similar course across different cultures?

Towards a Theory of Concept Formation

The traditional theory of concept formation, the theory of abstraction, is, therefore, mistaken on each of these three counts. The subject does not merely recognize resemblances among stimuli, since the subject's intentions and points of view help to determine that to which he responds. The formation of a concept is not adequately described as the development of a generalization from particular experiences, since there is no such thing as an absolutely particular experience: the existence of intentional consciousness means that we perceive things from a point of view, that is, as already being general, since the object of perception is an example of what we expect to find. And, finally, logico-mathematical concepts are not later derivations from physical experience, in the way that the traditional theory asserts; rather, they derive from the co-ordinations of our actions upon the world and are an essential part of our understanding of physical reality.

However, although the theory of abstraction is mistaken on each of these three counts, it must not be supposed that it is completely erroneous, so that our only remaining theoretical task is to develop a theory based upon the principles which oppose those of the traditional theory. For there is no doubt that the possession of a concept allows the subject to recognize resemblances among stimuli, that exposure to a variety of experiences is important in concept formation, and that the use of actual objects aids the development of logico-mathematical concepts. Therefore, in voicing opposition to this theory, we must be careful not to advocate a viewpoint which entirely opposes the traditional one and commits the opposing errors. We are led to the conclusion that the relationship between the terms of our analysis is not one of opposition but of complementarity. Intention informs attention, the general underlies the particular, and logico-mathematical knowledge is an essential component of physical knowledge. And these assertions are true for the same reason, namely, that the organization of reality and the development of concepts are correlative processes, two aspects of a single whole: our concepts develop as we organize the environment to which we respond and we organize our environment through developing our concepts; we know ourselves through knowing the world and we know the world through knowing our selves. Because of this, a concept is simultaneously the representation of a reality and the expression of an intention, a generalization from experience and an hypothesis, an organization of the stimulus and an act of co-ordination.

Our task is, then, still that of understanding how concepts develop through experience, but this critique implies a vastly different conception of experience than the abstractionist. All concepts, whatever developmental differences there might be, owe their existence to rules of relation, and it is the task of the psychology of concept formation to understand how these rules develop and are utilized. With simple, concrete concepts, the rule of relation is that of the resemblance of the elements, but there are other concepts which obey rules of relation other than that of classification: logical and mathematical concepts, for example, are not to be described simply in terms of the class concept. What is crucial in all forms of concept formation, as James, Cassirer, and Husserl all recognized, is that the identity of the generating relational rule is maintained throughout the formation.

Jenkins (1966) argued for the existence of three types of concept — concepts formed by abstraction of resemblances, concepts formed by a labelling response to perceptually dissimilar items, and concepts which are the expression of a rule. He remarked at one point that the first two types could probably be subsumed under the third, but he did not elaborate upon this point. A consideration of the criticisms made against the theory of abstraction shows, however, that it is essential that such an elaboration be carried out in order to arrive at a comprehensive and consistent theory of concept formation. The thesis is that all concepts owe their existence to the application of rules of relation ranging from the simple to the sophisticated. The idea of there being different kinds of concepts arises when one mistakenly focuses upon the end-product of well-established concepts, in which the rules of relation are implicit, rather than on the process of concept formation itself. It is evident that psychological studies of concept formation must escape from the limitations of the traditional theory of abstraction. In particular, it is suggested that this work ought to be guided by the following considerations and that a useful, psychological theory of the concept will be one that can encompass the following characteristics:

1. Concepts are the expression of the ways in which experience has become organized. Mathematical and logical concepts demonstrate this feature most clearly since they are rules by which elements may be related. But even the simplest concept is never just an observation, something merely registered by perception, for every concept presupposes a certain form of organization arising from the subject's intention. At the beginning,

this organization remains implicit, but intellectual development sees the emergence of explicit rules of relation (as we reflect upon our experience), of which the principle of classification is but one example.

2. All concepts are the result of particular instances becoming general by being treated as examples of a type or rule; further, language stabilizes these general meanings in the process of social interaction. However, concepts differ in the extent to which they embody truly general features of experience. At one extreme, logico-mathematical concepts may represent those operations which are common to all men, or potentially so, but at the other extreme are concepts which are strongly influenced by the peculiarities of the environment in which the individual develops. Thus, although we might reasonably expect both a Socialist and an Anarchist to have the same concept of subtraction, they will probably have different ideas about the concept of progress. Consequently, we require a theory of concept formation which will do justice to both the more personal and the potentially universal forms of concept.

3. Concepts are the result of acts of co-ordination. The existence of a rule of relation signifies that the elements subsumed by a concept are ordered by the same relation. In identifying a class of elements, the principle of similarity is utilized. To identify three points on a map or three people as forming a triangle means that the subject applies the same operations of proceeding from points A to B to C and then to A to qualitatively different elements. Or, to grasp the concept of subtraction means to understand the operations which are performed when subtracting. It is useful to distinguish physical concepts from logico-mathematical concepts, for the chief difference between these types is that in the former the rules of relation serve to structure the perceptible, whereas in the latter these rules develop into systems of operations which become detached from concrete reality to the extent that they can refer to any particular series of elements. However, these two types interact throughout development.

4. From the point of view of the subject, a concept is a disposition to organize events in a certain way and it implies the expectation that it is capable of being applied to fresh instances. In this sense, then, a concept is essentially predictive. In so far as a person is open to experiences that bear upon his concepts, these experiences will result in a modification of the concepts.

5. Since a concept is a result of the application of a rule to particular

elements, this can only mean that to study concept formation is to study the emerging correlation between such acts and the stimulus conditions to which they are related. It is false to begin with the assumption that there is, on the one hand, the thinking subject and, on the other, the "given" raw material which he has simply to interpret. For subject and environment are related in such a way that conceptual development is a process of making explicit what is implicit, of constructing one's concepts the more accurately the more they faithfully reflect the reality to which they refer. There is a reciprocal relationship between the interpretative acts by which we construct our models of reality and the properties of reality itself.

6. A concept may be defined, then, as a stable organization in the experience of reality which is achieved through the utilization of rules of relation and to which can be given a name.

CHAPTER 3

The Phenomenology of
Concept Learning

In the previous chapter I tried to argue that to regard consciousness as intentional in nature is to undermine all theories of concept formation from Locke to Wittgenstein that appeal to resemblances in the physical world as the sole basis for acts of categorization. Instead, it was suggested, the basis for categorization must be sought in the individual's motives for constructing his world — in what he is "intending" and aiming to predict. One implication of this viewpoint is that concept learning cannot be defined as the process of subsuming particulars under a general category, since this definition assumes that which it has to explain, namely, the formation of the general category, but must be seen as an act in which a stimulus comes to be taken as an instance of a type. In the present chapter I shall try to give more substance to this interpretation by recourse to phenomenology and particularly to the notion of tacit or pre-predicative knowledge.

Phenomenology is the discipline which is concerned with the systematic analysis of experience, so that the task of this chapter is to present an introduction to the phenomenology of concept learning. The approach to thinking from the vantage-point of conscious experience is, of course, in the tradition of philosophical or speculative psychology which reached its peak in the work of theorists such as William James, Husserl and Stout at the beginning of the present century. But I shall argue that these accounts are not merely of historical interest, that, on the contrary, it could be a valuable experience for those engaged at present in research on concept formation to consider these accounts and their relevance to experimental work. For it is surely not a question of opposing the analysis of experience to experimental psychology but of understanding how the two can be of mutual benefit.

The programme of the phenomenology elaborated by Husserl (1900, 1901, 1929) was nothing less than to understand the essential nature of the ways in which we experience reality. In order to accomplish this ambitious objective, it was deemed necessary to suspend or "put in brackets" all presuppositions and prejudices about experience of things and return "to the things themselves" or rather to the ways in which we actually come to know the things themselves. A few years before Husserl, James (1890) in his *Principles of Psychology* had argued in a similar vein and these two examinations of conscious experience, that of the philosopher seeking a firm basis for generalizations about human knowledge and that of the psychologist seeking to describe accurately the ways in which we experience the world, are strikingly similar. Both men were critical of traditional conceptions of consciousness which assumed that sensations and ideas were like atoms that could be associated without the elements themselves changing their nature and both stressed the unitary nature of consciousness. James saw clearly that every thought is, strictly speaking, unique and only resembles other thoughts of the same fact. For, "when the identical fact recurs, we *must* think of it in a fresh manner, see it under a somewhat different angle, apprehend it in different relations from those in which it last appeared" (p. 233). There is nothing in conscious experience answering the description of a permanently existing "idea" which occurs on different occasions in exactly the same form because consciousness does not consist of a large number of "elements". It does not appear to itself as chopped into bits but as flowing from one state into another. It is in this sense that James talked of the stream of consciousness, for one idea calls forth others, merges into them or stands out against them:

"What must be admitted is that the definite images of traditional psychology form but the very smallest part of our minds as they actually live. The traditional psychology talks like one who should say a river consists of nothing but pailsful, spoonsful, quartpotsful, barrelsful, and other moulded forms of water. Even were the pails and the pots all actually standing in the stream, still between them the free water would continue to flow. It is just this free water of consciousness that psychologists resolutely overlook. Every definite image in the mind is steeped and dyed in the free water that flows round it. With it goes the sense of its relations, near and remote, the dying echo of whence it came to us, the dawning sense of whither it is to lead" (1892, pp. 165—6).

Thus, there is no percept or thought which exists in isolation for each is surrounded by a "fringe" of other percepts and ideas. James argued that the difference between mere "acquaintance" with something and having knowledge of it is almost completely reducible to the absence or presence of psychic fringes. To be acquainted with something is to be limited to the bare impression which it makes, but to know a thing is to have knowledge of its relations. Here the author is clearly referring to different degrees of knowledge of something, for in acquaintance the relations between the central topic of thought and its implications are unarticulated and diffuse, whereas in true knowledge there is a more definite and harmonious relationship between the focal and the subsidiary aspects of thinking. According to James, the most important element of the fringes of consciousness is the feeling of harmony or discord, that is, the feeling that thought is progressing smoothly or in the wrong direction.

These ideas concerning psychic fringes and two kinds of knowledge illustrate the flow of consciousness but, equally fundamental, there is a sense of "sameness" which is at the root of concept formation. James (1890) refers to this sense as the "principle of constancy in the mind's meanings" (p. 459); this principle represents the fact that we can think of the same matter at different points in the flow of consciousness: through conception the mind can establish a permanent meaning which it can take up again and again. "The mind can always intend, and know when it intends, to think of the Same" (p. 459). It is the intention to think of the same objects again, and the awareness that we are doing so, that is the essential nature of conceptualization. The world of objects itself may be in constant flux but our intention to view the same object from a number of vantage-points can remain stable and succeed in endowing us with a mental structure which is usually called a concept. The concepts we form are, then, the consequence of the selectivity of attention (as we focus upon certain aspects of the stream of thought) and of the intention to hold fast to the meaning extracted. Hence, amidst the flux of sensations, opinions, and vague feelings, conceptions, which James defines as "things intended to be thought about" (p. 462), stand out as stable reference-points by which we succeed in gaining our bearings. Of course, this does not imply that any one thing can be conceived on different occasions in exactly the same state of mind, for this is logically impossible; the conception of an everyday object, such as an armchair, for example, is the same for me today as it was yesterday, but the very conception of it as the same is an additional complication to the thought. Thus, it is clear that the thoughts that we have of the same object are likely to be very different from one another, but the conception, that which we intend to think about, remains the same.

One of the major themes of the *Principles* is the selectivity of attention. From all the data which present themselves to the subject he selects certain aspects and these form the basis for his concepts of the world. There are two main determinants of the course of concept growth, the nature of the objects perceived by the subject, and the subject's intentions, purposes, and desires. Attention is selective because persons have specific interests and purposes to fulfil. This means that thinking is closely related to action, whether this is an overt activity or a covert activity such as is involved in logical or mathematical operations. There is in both cases a definite end to achieve and it is the awareness of the goal which sustains the thinking process through its course. Human purposes and interests are, of course, many and varied, but James thought that there are a smaller number of more important preoccupations and modes of thought which he referred to as sub-universes of reality. Nowadays, perhaps, we should refer to these as conceptual systems; they include the world of physical things, the world of science, of ideal relations, of the supernatural, and so forth. The task of understanding the nature of concepts in each of these systems and the ways in which they relate to one another or fail to do so is a topic taken up in the next chapter.

G. F. Stout

The English psychologist, G. F. Stout, took up James's ideas, although disagreeing with him over details. For instance, Stout held that James had not emphasized sufficiently the importance of psychic fringes for sense-perception. He pointed out (Stout, 1902) that the perception of any particular object involves reference to other objects or parts of a series which are not imagined explicitly but which nevertheless are important constituents of the percept:

"If I follow with my eye the movement of a body in space from one place to another, what I apprehend in sensible detail at any one moment is the changing position of the body at that moment. The successive phases of the process are imaged, but the movement as a whole cannot from the nature of the case be represented in sensuous detail. Besides actually perceiving or mentally envisaging the position of the object at this or that moment, I must, in order to be aware of the movement as a whole, have an anticipation of its future course, and a retrospect of its past course, in the way of imageless apprehension" (pp. 93–4).

What James called the fringe is, therefore, an indispensable part of perception as much as of thinking. Stout uses the term implicit apprehension, to refer to the apprehension of the whole that takes place without discernment of its parts. Either 'our apprehension of the whole is completely implicit, in which case there can be no synthesis of the parts, or apprehension can be partly explicit and partly implicit. So far as thinking goes, it is the implicit idea or perception of a whole which determines the "train of thought", the successive emergence of ideas into consciousness; it is therefore, a schematic apprehension, a general framework for the assimilation and integration of ideas.

Putting these conclusions in a slightly different form, it may be said that attention is always attention to some object and that it is the essential nature of the attention process that through it our apprehension of this object shall tend to become more full and distinct. Stout notes that "a certain prospective attitude of mind is characteristic of attention" (p. 184) and that this prospective attitude is mainly interrogative in quality. Attention is, then, "the growing-point of the mind" for it is the process through which cognitive systems develop. It is a mental adjustment to conditions which are not perfectly familiar; what arouses attention is neither familiarity nor unfamiliarity but the intermixture of the two. The activity of adjusting to such conditions as part of the process of developing cognitive systems is called *apperception*. Stout draws the analogy with the disturbance of equilibrium within a physical system which "acts" to restore stability. He says that attention itself corresponds to the series of occurrences, whether viewed from the cognitive or a physiological point of view, by which equilibrium is regained.

Phenomenology

It is evident that the ideas propounded by James and Stout are similar, and identical in many respects, to the conclusions of phenomenology and Gestalt psychology. In the previous chapter Husserl's notions of intentionality, the sense of identity in the flow of consciousness, and the concept of horizon were outlined. Each of these concepts has its equivalent in the psychologies of James and Stout. It is noteworthy, as Spiegelberg (1965) points out, that James discusses the sense of sameness in connection with the doctrine that there are two types of knowledge, *knowledge by acquaintance* and *knowledge about*, and this is paralleled in Husserl's work and in later phenomenological accounts by the distinction between *pre-predicative* and *predicative knowledge*. It may ¬ot be too fanciful, also, to suggest that very much the same meaning is expressed by Stout's distinction between awareness which is completely implicit and apprehension which is partly explicit and partly implicit.

From the phenomenological point of view the problem of concept learning is to understand how the subject can advance from knowledge by acquaintance to knowledge about, from a hazy and tacit understanding to a clear and articulated knowledge. It must be noted, however, that this process cannot be characterized as a transition from the merely implicit to the exclusively explicit, because all our ideas, no matter how conscious we are of them, have horizons which are not fully specifiable in advance of our using them. Let us go back to the distinction between the object of perception, defined as the object which the perceiving subject is aware of and intends, and the act of perception or of attention itself, the former being called the *noema*, the latter the *noesis*. Remember that Husserl laid great emphasis on the idea that we can experience the same object throughout the course of executing many different attentional acts: looking at a tree from a number of different angles and on a number of occasions, I am aware of the distinction between my acts of attending and the tree itself, which maintains its identity throughout. Generalizing from this, we may conclude that a conscious act always presents the subject who experiences it with a *sense*, an ideal unity of experience which remains the same over time. The exercise of consciousness, therefore, confronts the subject with senses which, since they retain their identity, he is free to call upon and utilize an indefinite number of times. There are intentional structures corresponding to perceptual objects, conceptual groupings or syntactic structures: in all of these cases the intentional functioning of consciousness has generated a permanent and objective meaning, objectivity being defined as the independence of the object of the mode of its apprehension. But, of course, we never experience an isolated object: my perception of the tree is charged with potentialities which may be revealed by further acts of exploration; the concept I am attending to at the moment is embedded in a whole series of both equally well defined concepts and more diffuse perceptions, images, and notions. The very way in which the concept of horizon is described necessitates reference to temporal succession, for the actual percept or concept is grounded in the results of a series of previous objectivating acts and points implicitly towards further acts.

For Merleau-Ponty (1962), the kind of intentionality which characterizes pre-predicative awareness is *motor intentionality*, which may be defined as the horizon of possible actualization of experience through bodily movement. It is the expressive power of bodily movements which enables the individual to situate himself within the world and orientate himself towards the possible since it is the body which provides him with a way of naturally expressing the motor intentions called up by contact with the environment. It is in this sense that Merleau-Ponty states that the primary fact of consciousness is not "I think", the thinking being divorced from action, but "I can". This is especially apparent when we compare normal with abnormal subjects. Merleau-Ponty devotes a large part of his analysis in the *Phenomenology of Perception* to a discussion of one of Goldstein's patients, named Schneider, who had been wounded by a shell splinter at the back of his head. If this patient is asked to move his arm, with no detailed instructions as to how, he is first of all perplexed; then he moves his whole body, and after a time his movements become confined to his arm, which he thus "finds". If he is asked to draw a circle or a square in the air, he first "finds" his arm, then lifts it in front of him, and finally makes a few rough movements in a straight line or describing various curves: if one of these happens to be circular, he promptly completes the circle. In using his body to perform a movement, then, he is like a speaker who has to follow a test before he can speak. There is no doubt that he understands the order, because he recognizes the inadequacy of his first attempts and, if he fortuitously produces the right movement,

he is capable of capitalizing upon it. The peculiar limitation to the subject's ability is that the instruction has only an *intellectual* significance for
him and not primarily a *motor* significance. What he lacks, argues Merleau-
Ponty, is neither motility nor thought but "something between movement
as a third person process and thought as a representation of that movement — something which is an anticipation of, or arrival at, the objective
and is ensured by the body itself as a motor power or motor intentionality"
(p. 110). This patient behaves as if he had no direct, first-hand awareness
of his body and the ways in which it may be employed to explore the
environment, but for the normal person every bodily movement is both
movement and consciousness of movement. The normal person is able to
operate upon the world, perceptually and conceptually, because his intentions polarize the world, establish perspectives, lines of force, horizons and
boundaries, but for a patient like Schneider the world appears to exist at a
distance from his own activity so that his problem-solving behaviour
strikes one as being excessively "intellectual": he must reason where we
can take for granted.

Schneider solves problems by attempting to subsume particular items of
information under explicit categories. Presented with a fountain pen in
such a way that the clip is not seen, he notes the attributes of the object
one at a time: "it is black, blue, and shiny; there is a white patch on it, and
it is rather long; it has the shape of a stick . . .". The pen is turned around
revealing the clip: "It must be a pencil or a fountain pen" (he touches his
breast pocket). "It is to put there, to make notes with." Merleau-Ponty
comments that in this example the sense-data are limited to suggesting
these meanings in the way that facts suggest hypotheses to the scientist.
The patient, like the scientist, proceeds to clarify his thought by cross-
checking facts against hypotheses. But this is not the way in which we normally think. In normal thinking we are able to make tacit use of acquired
knowledge without having to resort to explicit conceptual analysis. This
is because we are able to relate our present intentions to our past experience and this past experience is only really at our disposal as long as
our intentions are active and spontaneous:

"Similarly my acquired thoughts are not a final gain, they continually draw their sustenance from my present thought, they offer me a
meaning, but I give it back to them. Indeed our available store expresses for ever afresh the energy of our present consciousness.

Sometimes it weakens, as in moments of weariness, and then my 'world' of thought is impoverished and reduced to one or two obsessive ideas; sometimes, on the other hand, I am at the disposal of all my thoughts and every word spoken in front of me then stimulates questions and ideas, recasting and reorganizing the mental panorama, and presenting itself with a precise physiognomy. Thus what is acquired is truly acquired only if it is taken up again in a fresh momentum of thought, and a thought is assigned to its place only if it takes up its place itself" (Merleau-Ponty, 1962, p. 130).

On this view, therefore, to understand something is to be aware that an intention has been fulfilled; it is to experience the harmony between what is intended and what is experienced as "given". To learn a concept is to add a further cognitive structure to one's repertoire and at the same time to understand more about the environment to which that concept refers. There are, perhaps, three essential features of this perspective. In the first place, the truth of the concept, that is, the extent to which it reflects reality, is always partial because it rests upon the results of previous experience and upon presuppositions which are never made fully explicit. Secondly, conceptual knowledge, as other forms of knowledge (the enactive or the perceptual) rests upon what can only be described as acts of personal commitment, upon your or my willingness to take up the challenge of testing intentions against objects; it is this capacity for deploying intentions which, as Merleau-Ponty puts it, "goes limp" in illness, so that the world appears two-dimensional and all too familiar because it is not polarized and diversified by our interests in it. And finally, although the concept may be characterized as a cognitive structure, it is primarily a form taken by an *act* of interpretation; the link between conception and action is thus a close one and we can understand how it is possible to have several types of understanding of a concept, from the enactive to the contemplative.

The problem facing an explanation of concept learning is to explain how such intentional experience can generate new categories for the assimilation of reality. If all our knowledge consisted of explicit categories, then this problem would resist solution since we would either know something, in which case the problem does not arise, or we would not know it at all, so that we could not learn anything new. But once it is granted that all knowledge is not explicit and that, on the contrary, my awareness of something is always surrounded by a horizon of possibilities which remain to be explored by further acts of attention, then it becomes possible to acknowledge that what Polanyi (1959, 1967) calls tacit awareness may guide us to the discovery of new categories. It must be by a process of attending to stimuli that are not fully defined and articulated but which exist as the as yet unexplored horizon of more clearly articulated stimuli that the subject succeeds in advancing his conceptual understanding. The new concept thus emerges, not as some quite distinct and independent development, but as an extension of existing knowledge – a possibility that has been actualized. This explanation of the continuity of concept learning may be regarded as complementary to the equilibration hypothesis which similarly implies a progression in learning rather than the piecemeal accumulation of distinct concepts.

But, of course, it is only a preliminary statement as far as an explanation goes. In fact very little is known about the conditions which promote the use of stimuli existing at the level of tacit awareness in concept learning. And surely it is here that phenomenology might be able to interact profitably with experimental psychology. Because, in order to understand how the subject comes to utilize information which he initially regards as peripheral and subsidiary to his main line of thought, it is necessary to know more, through experimental manipulation, of the stimulus conditions which facilitate or impede this utilization. We need to understand the relationship between the properties of an on-going activity that is central to the subject's attention and subsidiary lines of thought and perception which accompany the central activity. This relationship, if phenomenological accounts are correct, is a two-way process, for the horizon of attention, the "ground" in Gestalt psychology, is as important in the constitution of the whole as is the central topic or figure. Such analyses raise some interesting questions for experimentation. What is the relative effectiveness of information presented for direct learning and information presented for incidental learning in concept formation? What kind of information is best presented for incidental learning and what for direct learning? What, if any, is the typical sequence for a concept learning task involving subsidiary and direct learning? Are some subjects consistently better at utilizing information presented for incidental learning and, if so, what other characteristics do they possess?

Although at present these questions have hardly received any experimental consideration, there is some evidence to suggest that there are stages in concept learning which correspond to phases of incidental and direct learning. Rommetveit (1961, 1965) has attempted to co-ordinate the two competing views of concept learning that we encountered in the Introduction, the "composite-photograph theory" which regards concept learning as an incidental activity in which sense impressions gradually summate to form a concept, and the "hypothesis-testing theory", which states that subjects search actively for support for hypotheses. He proposed that these apparently conflicting theories are in fact complementary because they reflect different phases of the process of concept learning. At the first phase, which Rommetveit terms *pre-functional*, the defining attributes of perceptual displays acquire distinctiveness, although the subjects are not yet able to sort them into appropriate conceptual categories. In Polanyi's terminology this is the stage of tacit learning. During the second phase distinctive modes of responding become associated with the defining attributes of the concept, that is, a *discriminatory, instrumental response* is established. And at the third phase the subject is able to represent *symbolically* the discrimination he has made. It is readily apparent that this theory is very similar to the notions of Bruner *et al.* (1966) about ikonic, enactive and symbolic modes of representation, although in Rommetveit's theory the ikonic stage, rather than the enactive, comes first. In a series of experiments (Rommetveit, 1965, Rommetveit and Kvale, 1965a, 1965b) which involved varying the training which subjects received – passive attention, instrumental responding, verbal labelling – the investigators were able to present some support for the three-stage theory. Asking their subjects to sort geometric figures into "good" and "bad" ones, they found the prefunctional stage under conditions of passive attention but not when subjects were told explicitly that they would be asked what "good" and "bad" patterns would be like, nor when subjects received prior training in observing and labelling systematically the geometrical properties of the patterns. Rommetveit argued that the subject's attention must not be directed at the discriminatory activity if the pre-functional stage is to manifest itself. However, from her experiments, Stenild (1972) suggested that this formulation is not entirely accurate. Her conclusion is worth quoting in full, since it sums up the argument pursued in this chapter:

"The theory is now that the activity in the first stage in concept learning can be characterized as intentionally directed at identifying the defining properties of the concept to be learned. The activity has to be characterized as intentional in the same way as for the two following stages. The first stage can further be characterized as a *hypothesis making* stage in which the individual is using a global strategy of scanning. Thus, the prerequisite for the manifestation of such a first stage is that the attention of the individual has to be directed at the discriminatory activity, but one must not demand specific reactions from the subject — one must not ask for an immediate categorizing activity" (p. 107).

Presumably, asking the subject to categorize initially inhibits the likelihood of global scanning. This latter is not characterized by an absence of direction and intention; rather, it is as though the intentional aspects of experience become subsidiary to the attentional.

Much more work is needed, however, before our understanding of the experience of concept learning can advance to clarity. Here, it seems, is an opportunity for work which can combine experimental rigour and ingenuity with a sensitivity to the characteristics of experience.

CHAPTER 4

Conceptual Systems

An account of the theoretical basis for the study of concept formation would be incomplete without some consideration of the nature of conceptual systems. This chapter will not be concerned with the exploration of the conceptual systems of different individuals along the lines of, for example, Personal Construct Theory (Kelly, 1955) or the Semantic Differential technique (Osgood, Suci and Tannenbaum, 1957). Both these approaches provide insight into the attitudes of subjects towards concepts that are selected because of their relevance to the person's life or because of the psychologist's particular interests. Important though these concerns are, the focus of the present chapter will be on an issue which has been somewhat neglected in psychology, its analysis owing more to the efforts of novelists, philosophers and sociologists than to academic psychologists. The problem, briefly outlined, is this: are there grounds for believing that concepts and conceptual systems necessarily divide into different types according to the psychological processes involved in their formation and use? In other words, are there several modes of thinking, and not just one, and, if so, what is the proper way of describing the relationship between them? Psychologists have paid little attention to these questions and they have generally defined the concept in such a way as to preclude the possibility that there are different kinds of concept. This criticism is valid in relation to the traditional definition which equates a concept with a class of objects or events and which, therefore, presupposes that concepts are arranged in systems that obey the rules of classification. It is valid, also, with respect to Kelly's (1955) definition of the construct as a means of dividing reality into opposites, such as "black-white" or "pleasant-unpleasant". These definitions are limiting because it may well be that not all concepts are classificatory or bi-polar. On the other hand, according to the definition presented in this account of concept formation that a concept is a stable organization of experience which can be named and which is brought about through the application of a rule of relation, it may be allowed that there are different types of experience, each with its own characteristic set of concepts and each having the stability of its own peculiar form of organization. We are then in a position to ask how, for example, aesthetic concepts differ from scientific concepts or our conceptions of the everyday world from those of religion. Or we can inquire into the differences between concepts attributed to people, such as "moral—immoral" or "sincere—insincere", and those attributed to objects or to the objective characteristics of people. The first question that must be answered, then, is: are there different types of concepts? Having attempted an answer to this question, we can raise the question of the nature of conceptual systems.

Types of Concept

There are, perhaps, three major types of concept which require specific definitions over and above the general definition of the concept. Two of these have already appeared in an earlier chapter (p. 18), namely, physical concepts and logico-mathematical concepts. To these is to be added a third type, which, following Collingwood (1933), will be called philosophical concepts. It may be recalled that the distinction between physical and logico-mathematical concepts lies in the former referring to properties inherent in objects and the latter referring to the structures inherent in those actions which are co-ordinated and internalized to become operations. It is maintained, after Piaget, that these two kinds of experience interact in the course of development; this means that the subject develops an understanding of the world of objects at the same time as he is forming operational structures. Physical experience is necessary for the development of operational knowledge, since it provides the medium — at first concrete but later symbolized — through which operations develop, but, equally, operational competence is necessary for the understanding of reality, since we would not know very much about the properties of objects without the means of ordering and relating them. But there is a third type of concept, which we have not yet considered, that has to do neither with the properties of objects nor with properties of operations. This third type of concept is most in evidence when we have cause to refer to personal qualities. Let us examine Collingwood's (1933) definition of this type of concept to understand its peculiar nature and the reason for it being called philosophical.

He noted that the traditional definition of the concept as a class of objects with a common property is valid enough with respect to the exact concepts gained through deduction in logic and mathematics and also with respect to empirical knowledge gained through induction: thus, a line is either straight or curved and an animal is a member of one species and not another. It is true that there may be border-line cases which are difficult to fit into the classificatory framework, but these exceptions do not challenge the principle of classification or the particular classificatory structure. However, classification and division cannot be applied to what Collingwood calls philosophical concepts because the overlap of classes is such as to challenge the very principles of classification. There are countless examples of these concepts as soon as one begins to examine the nature of human experience. For example, philosophers traditionally divide what is "good". into three species — the pleasant, the expedient, and the right — but no one could seriously maintain that these are mutually exclusive species obeying principles of classification, for this would imply that whatever is pleasant must therefore be inexpedient and wrong, or that whatever is expedient must be both wrong and unpleasant. If these types were mutually exclusive, then a man could not enjoy doing what is right or believe that actions are right in so far as they promote happiness. Clearly, we are dealing here with properties which it makes sense to distinguish but which do not conform to the rules of classification. Or take the question of the motivation of behaviour. It is possible, no doubt, to draw up a list of the different kinds of motives, but who could deny that in many instances of behaviour motives are many and mixed. Similarly, thought and action are distinguishable but in their existence in concrete instances they are so connected that it is possible for an instance of one to be an instance of the other also: we do talk of acting rationally and of thinking resolutely.

Not all psychological concepts present these peculiar difficulties; it is only when such concepts enter into "a philosophical phase" that they do so. Collingwood points out, for instance, that when sensation is divided into seeing, hearing, and so forth, then consideration of the separate species can be left to psychologists and physiologists. It is only those psychological concepts which demonstrate the overlap of classes which are of philosophical interest and which constitute a different type. In order to understand the structure of this type of concept, we must first distinguish between differences of kind and differences of degree. The overlap of classes cannot be due to difference in degree between properties since there are definite boundary lines in a series so formed (for example, a classification of men by age for military service). Nor can it be explained as being due to differences in kind, for again there are clearly differentiated species. Rather, what characterizes philosophical concepts is that differences in degree exist in combination with differences in kind in what Collingwood calls "a scale of forms". In a scale of forms there is both a difference in kind between the various forms which embody the essential element in the concept and a difference in the degree to which these forms embody it. The concept of intelligence viewed in a Piagetian perspective constitutes a scale of forms since intelligence is seen as existing at different levels which differ both in degree and in kind: thus, the concrete operational level represents a higher form of intelligence than the pre-operational level but it also differs from it in kind, being qualitatively different. Collingwood provides numerous examples of concepts which follow the same pattern:

"Where one work of art is more beautiful than another, no great subtlety of thought is needed to recognize that it is beautiful in a different way; it does not merely exceed the other, for the other has its own kind of beauty, and can only be beaten by one which achieves a beauty of a higher kind. Thus, it is not wholly true that there are degrees of beauty, if this means that beauty differs from beauty not in kind but only in degree; nor is it true that there are no such degrees, if this means that the kinds of beauty are all perfect each in its own way; for they are different in degree as well as in kind, so that the beauty of a comic epigram, however perfect, is not only the beauty of a small thing compared with the *Iliad* but is a lesser as well as a different beauty.

"The same is true of pleasure, goodness, and the other concepts belonging to the sphere of philosophy. Hastily considered, they may seem to obey the traditional rules of specification, modified by an overlap of classes; more closely scrutinized, they always reveal this characteristic fusion of differences in degree with differences in kind" (Collingwood, 1933, pp. 77–78).

Philosophical concepts are, therefore, not to be confused with concepts based upon the principles of classification, which refer to differences in kind, or with concepts based upon opposition between two attributes, between which there are degrees of difference, for their distinguishing feature is that each concept forms or is part of a series which proceeds from lower to higher levels in a manner in which differences in degree are combined with differences in kind. Further, they are distinct from both logico-mathematical and physical concepts, since these refer respectively to the structures evident in operations and in physical reality, whereas philosophical concepts arise whenever we reflect upon the intrinsic significance of our experience, that is, when we try to determine what it means to be "more intelligent" or "emotionally mature" or "moral", "beautiful", and so forth. It should not then be supposed that labelling these concepts "philosophical" necessarily reduces them to a specialized and narrow field of application, for all of us, in so far as we are capable of reflection upon our experience, have to do with concepts of this kind. Just as the description of logico-mathematical and physical experience amounts to both a delineation of psychological structures (concepts) and of the reality which these structures refer to (the structures of actions and of physical reality), so a description of philosophical concepts involves a dual reference to ideas and to an underlying reality which we are attempting to understand more clearly. But, as soon as we begin to reflect upon the philosophical significance of experience, it becomes apparent that significance can be found within a number of conceptual systems and that there is no concensus of opinion on the scale of forms appropriate to these systems: some claim that the values and methods of Science should be dominant, others claim the same privilege for Art or Religion. The same questions must, therefore, be asked of conceptual systems as were asked of conceptual types: what are the major forms in which concepts are grouped together and how may the relationship between these forms be described?

Conceptual Systems

But what grounds have we for asserting that there are several conceptual systems, each with its own manner of defining what reality is? Surely, it may be reasoned, there is only one reality and each person has a set of concepts, loosely related though they may be, for apprehending it. We are not normally aware of discrepant realities and our lives are not so sharply partitioned that we experience a sense of shock when we pass from one kind of activity to another. Now, all this is perfectly true: there is a world of everyday reality, which has been termed the "taken-for-granted-world" (Schutz, 1966) or the world of "practical realities" (James, 1890), that is of paramount importance in the normal course of events because it allows life to be lived without too many troublesome questions. But the matter cannot be left there, because, first, the maintenance of everyday reality depends upon the suppression of alternative perspectives which are likely to challenge it, and, secondly, because these perspectives themselves not only conflict with the world of common sense but also appear to be inconsistent with one another. Given the truth of these two assertions, the important question is whether this inconsistency *is* only apparent and can therefore be resolved.

William James (1890) saw clearly that there are various categories of reality and illusion: there are the worlds of abstract reality, of practical reality, of ideal relations (as in logic and mathematics), of superstition, and of madness. He noted that ordinarily we conceive all these sub-worlds disconnectedly and avoid inconsistency when dealing with one of them by forgetting about the others. The sociologist, Alfred Schutz (1966), has elaborated the same theme, asserting that to live a normal life in society, reality must be taken for granted as such. This requires a suspension of any doubts about the nature of that reality, because only then does reality take on the appearance of an orderly progression. Berger (1970) has pointed out that Robert Musil's novel, *The Man Without Qualities*, constitutes an extensive exploration of ideas similar to those propounded by James and Schutz. The maintenance of the world of everyday reality depends, according to Musil, upon "a perspectival abridgment of consciousness", a shortening of perspectives which goes some way towards ensuring that our lives have a definite course. From within its own perspective, everyday reality assigns to the other realities the status of "utopias": the worlds of art, religion or science are seen, at best, as interludes which conveniently divide the paramount reality of everyday life. But this continuity is a trick and an illusion. When we inquire more closely into this world, it loses its taken-for-granted character and itself takes on the appearance of a utopia — a highly artificial and rather unlikely drama.

The events described in Musil's novel take place in the year 1913. Although the novel is concerned not with actual events leading up to the outbreak of the First World War but with ideas and how these are embodied in the lives of those living at this time, the reader is aware of the contrast between the uncertainty and the provisional nature of these ideas and the massive, impending certainty of the War. This contrast is sharply defined in one of the central events of the novel, the formation of a committee which has the specific purpose of finding a suitable intellectual theme for the celebration of the Austrian Emperor's jubilee in 1918. The search for this theme becomes the search for "a unifying idea" which will summarize the achievements of the Austrian Empire and its place in the contemporary world. Since the committee invites suggestions from various quarters as to what this idea might be, the project can only be a reflection of the numerous and conflicting ideas and ideologies which are at play in everyday reality: it is, therefore, in the words of the central character of the novel, the man who has decided to forgo his personal qualities until he can discover the proper conditions for their use, one of those projects that exist only in order to state their own unreality, for it is inevitable that no unifying idea will be found. Perhaps the most entertaining representation of the chaos that follows is provided by General Stumm von Bordwehr, a member of the military attached in some vague way to the committee in order to see that the Army's interests are safeguarded. Although this may appear to be a sinister mission, the general is a most likeable fellow who earnestly sets about trying to unravel the mysteries of the civilian mind. After much deliberation, he decides that the best way of accomplishing this objective is to represent the major ideas (Christianity, Marxism, Idealism, etc.) by means of a sort of battle-plan so that he can discover the major patterns among them. But, after employing a captain, two lieutenants, and five N.C.O.s on the preparation of these ideological maps, he observed with some dismay that any one of the idea-units received its supply of fighting troops and intellectual war-material not only from its own bases but also from those of its enemy.

"You will see that it is continually shifting positions and, suddenly, without any cause, it turns its front and fights against its own lines of communication. And then again you will see that the ideas are ceaselessly going over to the enemy, and then back again, so that you will find them now in one, now in another line of battle" (vol. 2, p. 89).

The attempt to apply the precise logic of military strategy to the ideas which we refer to in order to justify one belief rather than another can only lead to a sense of frustration:

" 'I have tried a lot more experiments of various kinds,' the General said, and in his gay and lively eyes there was now a faint gleam of irritation or even panic, 'trying to get the whole thing reduced to unity. But d'you know what it's like? Just like travelling second-class in Galicia and picking up fleas! It's the lousiest feeling of helplessness I ever knew. When you've been spending a lot of time among ideas, you get an itching all over your body, and you can't get any peace even if you scratch till you bleed!' " (Musil, 1953, vol. 2, p. 90).

Upon reflection, then, the world of common sense loses its taken-for-granted character and itself becomes precarious and problematic. We become aware of this when we move from one province of meaning to another. Musil refers to such transitions as "border line experiences", in which we become aware of the assumptions of the natural attitude and, simultaneously, of the possibility of more authentic modes of existence. For, in putting aside the presuppositions of common sense, one abolishes a firm sense of reality since it becomes clear that there is no secure basis for consistency among competing conceptual systems, no "rallying-point" that would bring sense and coherence to human activities which are meaningful in themselves but devoid of meaning as a whole. Further, given that there are a number of realities, the abstract and genuinely scientific question of how the experiences related to these realities are to be described and explained with respect to one another is equivalent to the concrete, existential question of how I may live my life as a coherent whole. If it is maintained that these issues exceed the boundary line of psychology as a scientific discipline, since the psychologist is concerned with how life *is* and not with how it *should be*, it can only be replied that this argument conveniently forgets the nature of the subject as a human being; it is forgotten that the subject is concerned with justifying his behaviour and experience to himself and to others, and these various justifications are themselves part of the factual material of the discipline.

James lists the most important sub-universes as follows:

1. The world of sense, or of physical things as we instinctively apprehend them.
2. The world of science, or of physical things as the learned conceive them.
3. The world of ideal relations or abstract truths believed or believable by all, and expressed in logical, mathematical, ethical, metaphysical, and aesthetic propositions.
4. The world of "idols of the tribe", illusions or prejudices common to the race.
5. The various supernatural worlds, for example, the Christian Heaven and Hell or the world of Greek mythology.
6. The various worlds of individual opinion, "as numerous as men are".
7. The worlds of sheer madness, "also indefinitely numerous".

James believed that every object we think of is ultimately referred to one of these worlds, but these worlds appear to most men's minds in no definitely conceived relation to one another. Propositions are made from different points of view and the consciousness of most thinkers remains in this chaotic state to the end. He says that these different realities correspond to our different needs and whatever answers to these is treated as real, but he does not examine seriously the notion that there is also a strong need for consistency among ideas, nor does he raise the possibility that there is some necessary order among these realities because of the way in which the mind functions.

With this question we are ourselves upon the threshold of a "borderline experience" in respect to the frontier between Philosophy and Psychology. The problem of multiple realities has been faced squarely in Anthropology (see, for example, the debate reported in Horton and Finnegan's *Modes of Thought*) and in the sociology of knowledge (Schutz, 1966). Whether there are universal criteria of truth which transcend particular cultures and the modes of thought characteristic of them or whether there are fundamental incompatibilities between competing realities is very much a contemporary question. For the student of concept formation the question itself is a reminder of the possible contingency of his own definitions of the concept. Sooner or later, if he is to do justice to the variety of modes of thought and to the need for coherence, this particular nettle will have to be grasped.

PART II

CONCEPTUAL
DEVELOPMENT

CHAPTER 5

Pre-Conceptual Developments

Introduction

A definition is useful if it delineates an area of study. We have defined the concept as a stable organization of experience which is brought about through the application of a rule of relation and to which is assigned a particular name. Our area of study is defined by the three components of this definition. To say that the concept is a particular organization of experience suggests that one point of departure must be a consideration of the development of concepts from their roots in the achievements of perceptual organization; to say that it is brought about through an act of relation implies that we must look also to the achievements of sensori-motor intelligence as preparing the way for conceptual development; and to say that the concept is characterized by there being an agreed name for the experience means that language plays an indispensible role in concept formation. In this chapter, therefore, we shall be concerned with the antecedents of true conceptual development with especial reference to perceptual, sensori-motor and linguistic processes.

One implication of this reasoning is that it is quite impossible to set a lower limit to conceptual development. Before the child begins to employ concepts in understanding his environment, he is capable of organization of the perceptual field, of acting intelligently upon objects, and even of using language to express feelings and to denote objects. What is called a concept is, then, the consequence of a whole series of antecedent developments. It is in this sense that it may be asserted that the conceptual organization of reality is implicit in pre-conceptual organization since the latter is an interpretation of reality just as much as the former. Because the development of thinking and the growth of sensitivity to the environment are parallel processes, accommodation to the properties of the environment always presupposes some act of interpretation, however rudimentary, and every interpretation contains some measure of reality-orientation, however slight. Theorists are mistaken, therefore, who distinguish sharply between behaviour which is merely associative and that which is cognitive (i.e. interpretative), assigning to the former a lower developmental stage. It may well be that some tasks are more associative and others more cognitive, but it is quite false to conclude from this that there are two developmental levels, at one of which behaviour is governed solely by random associations. We shall see that there is no empirical justification for this view and there is no theoretical justification either, since, if interpretation were not somehow inherent in sensori-motor behaviour, there would be an unbridgeable discontinuity between the sensori-motor and the conceptual levels of development.

One of the most fundamental questions in connection with these early developments has to do with the problem of describing the interaction of the relevant variables. Consider, for example, the relationship between language development and the internalization of actions into systems of operations. It seems likely that the two are initially independent, language at first referring ambiguously to external objects and to the child's own feelings, and the first internalizations of actions being either imitative of the properties of objects or playful exercising of existing schemes without genuine adaptation, but that at some point in development language becomes co-ordinated with the child's ability to structure his environment through acts of relating; that is, instead of the child merely co-ordinating objects he can co-ordinate symbols of objects. But it seems unlikely that we are dealing with two entirely different lines of development which simply come together at some point in development. Just as it must be assumed that there is an implicit conceptual activity in preconceptual development, so it must also be accepted that some features of language use are implicit in early sensori-motor co-ordinations, so that language must be traced back to these, and conversely, that some features of sensorimotor intelligence are present in the first use of language. We are not dealing with independent variables, therefore, because there are structural similarities between language and thinking.

Stated in the most general terms, development towards the use of concepts involves two principles which, understood superficially, appear to conflict. The first is that development brings about an increasing differentiation of the subject from his environment: the formation of the general concept depends upon the child freeing himself from the distorting influences of immediate stimulation, both from without and within. Freedom from the immediate here-and-now is essential in order that stable concepts can be formed. They are stable because they reflect enduring aspects of the real world. The child in the preconceptual period learns more about his environment by being able to detach himself from it so as to observe the better its effects and differentiate these from the effects of his own actions, and more about himself through acquiring the ability to differentiate between his own desires and inclinations on the one hand and actual events and states of affairs on the other. It is this process which ensures, in the normal course of development, that concepts, when formed, can be used by the individual as predictions which are grounded in the reality he has experienced. There is, therefore, no incompatibility between the idea that development involves an increasing freedom of response from immediate stimulation, and the second principle that development brings about an increasing correspondence between stimulation and response, since this correspondence is achieved through progressive differentiation between subject and environment.

The Identity of Objects

One of the most significant achievements of this period of development is the formation of a sense of the identity and permanence of objects. The infant behaves at first as though he believed that there are no permanent objects, as though there was not one object or person who appeared at different times or places but a number of objects corresponding to the occasions when they appeared (Piaget, 1951; Bower, 1971).

How does the infant progress from a world such as this to one populated by permanent objects? To understand this process we must note, first, that the difference between the earliest developmental levels and those later ones which are judged to involve orientation to reality is one of degree. The two major developmental theories are in agreement on this issue. Freud (1915) distinguished between primary and secondary processes on the grounds that the former are governed by the pleasure principle, the latter by the reality principle. In primary process thinking relations between ideas are determined by the nature of the individual's desires, whereas in secondary process thinking relationships between ideas are under the control of the desire of the individual to adapt to his environment. According to Freudian theory the study of dreams provides insight into the nature of the primary processes, for in dreams the demands of reality and of convention are subverted: actual things and events are distorted as they are utilized in a narrative which corresponds, albeit often obscurely, to the needs and wishes of the dreamer. In the dream we see three main mechanisms: condensation, which is the combination or fusion of several actual images into one — Freud (1929) described this as a rudimentary concept since the different images are united through their having in common the same desire; displacement, which is the shifting of an emotion from its real-life object to another; and symbolization, which is defined as the substitution of one object as representative of another, for example, symbolizing birth by the image of water. Now, it is clear from this account that the primary process is not completely divorced from reality. As Gill (1967) has pointed out, in all primary process functioning the secondary processes provide the impetus and the initial content of the experience since the primary processes are operative only when the individual's desires cannot be immediately satisfied. The mechanisms of the primary process are, in reality, mechanisms brought into play when adaptation to the environment has to be delayed, and to this extent they contain some reality-orientation. Similarly, with respect to Piagetian theory, although assimilation and accommodation can be conceptually distinguished, it is apparent that the earliest mechanism, the reflex, which functions in a rigid manner and which therefore seems to qualify as pure assimilatory activity, does in fact involve a primitive form of accommodation to the demands of the object and, as Piaget has shown with respect to the sucking reflex, is capable of demonstrating an improvement in its accommodation to the object over the course of the first few weeks of life. It is not, therefore, a question of a mode of functioning which is not adapted to the environment being replaced by one that is, but rather a question of a mode which is adapted only in the most restricted of ways being replaced by others which suffer from progressively fewer restrictions.

By far the most important means of overcoming these limitations is provided by the increasing capacity of the child to act upon his environment. The transition from primary to secondary process occurs when the child substitutes a search for the desired object for the hallucination of it. The development of sensori-motor co-ordinations, of vision with grasping or of different types of movement themselves, for example, enables the infant to explore the properties of objects and thus to dissociate them from his own desires and acts upon them. The sequence identified by Piaget for the attainment of the notion of the permanent object is well known and has been confirmed by other investigators (Woodward, 1959; White, 1972). After the first period, in which the child, who observes an object disappear behind another, say, a cushion, behaves as though the object no longer existed (i.e. he loses interest in the object and is not distressed by its disappearance), there occurs a stage at which this limitation is overcome, for the child now searches for the object where it disappeared. However, the child's notion of the permanence of the object is still linked closely to his own activity. This can be demonstrated by allowing the child to recover the object from behind cushion A and subsequently hiding it behind a second cushion, B. The child at a certain stage in his development will continue to search for the object where he found it and will not search under B, although he has observed the object to disappear there. This limitation is overcome, according to Piaget, at about 12 months, but one further limitation remains: the child cannot as yet take into account invisible displacements of objects. This means that the child is only successful when he is able to observe all the successive displacements of the object, but when confronted by one which he has to imagine or represent, he fails to keep track of the object, as when, for instance, an adult pretends to transfer an object from one hand to another but in fact does not. This limitation is overcome at about 18 months and is one of the achievements which marks the beginning of a major new period in the development of intelligence since the child has acquired the ability to represent the object.

In parallel with these developments, the child has developed a greater ability to explore the properties of objects themselves. At first an object is simply assimilated into an existing scheme and little or no attention is paid to the unique characteristics of the object. But gradually the child's actions begin to accommodate more and more to the object's characteristics. This can be seen most clearly at that stage, from about 12 to 18 months, in which the child varies his actions in order to observe the effect of this variation upon the behaviour of the object. Thus, in hitting the table with a spoon he might "try out" the effects of different impetus or rhythms.

Such behaviour signifies progress in the differentiation of the subject and his environment and, as Werner and Kaplan (1963) point out, this differentiation is the necessary basis for the development of the symbolic function, which they define to occur at that point in development when the child passes from a world of "things-of-action", articulated in terms of affective, sensori-motor schemes, to a world of "objects-of-contemplation", organized by reference to the properties of objects. In this transition the developing child makes use of the sensori-motor schemes by which he has articulated the world up to that point, but now these patterns undergo a shift of function, for their purpose is now primarily that of allowing the child to become aware of the characteristics of objects, rather than being simply accompaniments to his own actions, so that symbol formation begins when the child feels the need to name objects. Werner and Kaplan argue that the earliest expressions consist mainly of denotative utterances expressing names of persons, objects or animals or feelings of delight or surprise, etc. The important cognitive ability underlying them is that of identifying, of isolating and articulating something.

Not only does the development of sensori-motor intelligence contribute to the development of the symbolic function through the process of differentiation of subject and environment, but there may also be structural similarities between sensori-motor intelligence and language. In other words, the rules of relation which are implicit in sensori-motor activity and which become progressively more complex may also underlie linguistic performance, so that there is, in a sense, some transfer of learning from the sensori-motor to the linguistic spheres. This idea is quite speculative but empirical work into the suggestions put forward by Sinclair-de-Zwart (1967) along these lines may help to clarify the question of the cognitive basis of language learning. She has pointed out that the sensori-motor achievements of ordering, classifying (i.e. using same action for a whole class of objects or applying a whole series of action schemes to same object), and relating objects and actions, have linguistic equivalents, for instance, ordering words in a sentence, categorization, and the use of functional grammatical relations, such as "subject of" or "object of".

However, although it is reasonable to suppose that there are such antecedents of language acquisition, language does not function perfectly efficiently from its first appearance but itself shows developmental changes which ensure that it is more adapted to the process of concept formation.

The Early Development of Language

The first words, which usually appear between 10 and 12 months, are often used to express a variety of meanings. They are most frequently nouns which can fulfil this function since they contain grammatical relations implicitly. Thus, a child might use the word "milk" to indicate that he wants milk, or to refer to the milk, or as a request that another person should look at the milk. Such speech is called *holophrastic* speech, for the word has the character of a whole phrase. There are perhaps three main characteristics of holophrastic speech (McNeill, 1970). In the first place, it is closely linked with action, so that at times action and speech appear to be fused: thus one child was observed to say "walk" whenever she got out of a cart, and "away" when she pushed an object away. Secondly, it may be expressive of some emotion, for instance when a child uses a word to express approval or annoyance. Finally, it may refer to things, the child identifying an object by giving it a name. The course of development in the child's use of single words is from the use of a word to express a variety of meanings to its use in the expression of one particular meaning. The fact that the word is linked at first with action and desire means that the child's use of language is initially a continuation of sensori-motor development but, as we have seen, the word also has the function of naming and identifying, and this fact signifies that there is some progress towards the formation of concepts. Such words are, therefore, intermediate between actions and concepts.

If the noun is to fulfil its function in concept formation of referring to objects or experiences or co-ordinations of actions etc., the grammatical relations which are implicit in the child's first use of nouns must be taken over by other parts of speech. Whilst a full description of this developmental process is beyond the scope of this book, it is necessary to consider the early phases of the process in order to understand how language becomes adapted to the needs of concept formation. The child's first two-word utterances usually appear at about 18 or 20 months and, in general, appear not to be just random combinations of words but, rather, to take on a particular form, in which there are two distinct types of words, referred to as *pivot* and *open-class* words. The pivot class is small and each word in it is used with many different words from the larger open class. "No" and "all-gone" are common pivot words; they can be used together with many open-class words, for example, when the child says "no shoe" or "allgone milk". It has been argued that, although a pivot word may be the first or second element in a two-word utterance, each pivot word has its own fixed position. While the pivot class consists of a small number of words which are frequently used, the open class is large and contains all the words in a child's vocabulary that are not in the pivot class; most of the early growth in vocabulary occurs in the open class.

The description of the child's first sentences by this pivot–open grammar no doubt contains a measure of truth, but the grammar suffers from serious limitations. The speech of some children cannot be described by a pivot–open grammar: some children do use a small stock of words frequently, but not in a fixed position, and, also, there are examples of pivot words occurring on their own, which, if they are pivot words, they should not. But perhaps more significant than these limitations is the fact that the grammar cannot adequately convey the complexity of meaning evident in these two-word utterances. Brown (1970) identifies twelve different structural meanings involved in the child's first sentences.

Fig. 5.1. The first sentences in child speech

Structural meaning	Form	Example
1. Nomination	that + N it + N	that book
2. Notice	hi + N	hi belt
3. Recurrence	more + N, 'nother + N	more milk
4. Nonexistence	allgone + N, no more + N	allgone rattle
5. Attributive	Adj + N	big train
6. Possessive	N + N	mommy lunch
7. Locative	N + N	sweater chair
8. Locative	V + N	walk street
9. Agent-Action	N + V	Eve ready
10. Agent-Object	N + N	mommy sock
11. Action-Object	V + N	put book
12. Conjunction	N + N	umbrella boot

Source: Adapted by P. S. Dale, *Language Development: Structure and Function.*

Werner and Kaplan (1963) maintain that the child's first two-word utterances are not greatly differentiated but that development sees the emergence of two-word sentences which do refer to two distinct objects or activities. The evidence they present for this contention is scanty. They point to examples from a few children of lack of differentiation at an early stage and more differentiated expressions at a more advanced. Thus, at the beginning the child may say "da-digda", where both "da" and "digda" refer to the total situation of the sounding clock, but he develops to using expressions such as "birdie whistles", in which the first unit refers predominantly to the bird and the second to the sound the bird makes. The two elements of the first example refer to the same global event and, therefore, the expression is not far removed from a holophrastic word, whereas the two elements of the second utterance emphasize relatively different features of the event. Werner and Kaplan argue that examples of this sort indicate that the two-word phase may not be a unitary stage but may encompass a series of steps in the development of speech.

In a previous chapter a concept was defined as the expression through an agreed symbol of a particular meaning. Now the traditional theory of language acquisition is that meaning is acquired through the association of words with objects. The child learns the word for rabbit by hearing the word spoken in the presence of the stimulus, whether a real rabbit or a picture of one. But that this theory is mistaken and needs to be replaced by one which recognizes the intentional nature of experience is evident on a moment's reflection. As Macnamara (1972), among others, has pointed out, the child's success in acquiring language cannot be due to his simply associating words with objects, because there would be just no possibility of the child isolating and identifying the meaning of a word in this way. Thus hearing the sound "rabbit" in conjunction with a picture of a rabbit, how is he to know whether the word refers to the whole rabbit, or a part of the animal, or some particular aspect of the picture? There are all kinds of possible associations but only certain conjunctions of word and object are in fact acquired. It seems much more likely, therefore, that the child learns the relations between words and objects through comprehending the intentions of the speaker towards the object. Very little is known about the development of such comprehension. Macnamara suggests that children first learn the names of whole objects, then names for their variable states, and finally names for the permanent attributes of objects. The development of the capacity to name whole objects ensures that the infant has a stable focal point before developing the skill of naming varying states and activities, and, having comprehended these, he can then proceed to attend to and name more permanent attributes. Whether this description is accurate or not, it is evident that the child's ability to use words to refer to different aspects of his experience is dependent upon the development of cognitive skills connected with both the differentiation of subjective desires and feelings from external reality and with the comprehension of the intentions of others towards that external reality. This generalization is, of course, also relevant to communication between adult speakers: we understand one another, not by a process in which words spoken by one elicit the same associations in another, but by a process in which there is an active attempt to understand the other's point of view. It has been suggested (Ryan, 1974; Howe, 1976) that researchers should focus upon the mutual process of interpretation that goes on between parent and child.

The Development of Mental Imagery

There is, however, a further development that occurs at about two years of age which has to be taken into account if we are to understand the advances the child makes towards forming concepts, namely, the appearance of mental imagery, defined as the capacity to evoke an image of an object in the absence of that object. While the concept, which refers to a general class of objects, relations, etc., is not to be confused with the image, which always remains specific and individual, nevertheless it seems likely that the two are related, the image being a concrete and the concept an abstract representation.

Piaget distinguishes two aspects of any act of knowing which he refers to as the *figurative* and the *operative* components (Piaget and Inhelder, 1971). Figurative knowledge is gained through the activity of accommodation to the properties of objects and therefore includes imitation (gestural, visual, auditory). Operative knowledge, on the other hand, is the outcome of some transformation and includes sensori-motor schemes and internalized actions as well as operations. Furth (1969) expresses the essential quality of figurative knowing when he says that "figurative knowledge does not transform a reality state, rather it modifies the organism according to the figural aspect of that state" (p. 135). According to this viewpoint the image arises from acts of visual accommodation in which the subject traces the outline properties of an object through eye movements. Piaget and Inhelder use the term *schema* to refer to an image so formed. In time the image is capable of functioning in the absence of the object and becomes a true mental image. It is evident that this theory of the image is opposed to the view that the image is merely an extension of perception and thus a copy of reality since it is the result of accommodatory activity.

The relationship between imagery and thought is still a matter of contention but, following Piaget and Inhelder (1971), we can distinguish three positions on this issue. One view is that the image is an essential element of thinking. This theory was, however, shown to be doubtful by experiments carried out by the Würzburg group at the beginning of the century, for these investigators found that thinking could proceed without subjects reporting any imagery. At the other extreme, there is the view that imagery is at best an auxiliary to thinking and then only occasionally useful. Piaget and Inhelder argue that there is room for a third viewpoint which ascribes to imagery a more important role without confusing image and thought. They ask:

"... Would it not be possible to view imaginal and intuitive representation, which stands in the place of operations at the levels where these are not yet formed, as the starting point of the personal and imaginal symbolism required by all adults in order to concretize the abstract thought related to verbal signs and mathematical language?" (p. 10).

They point out that this personal symbolism is particularly alive in mathematicians themselves and that those people who are able to handle abstractions successfully are often those who are best at embodying them in concrete examples. But, and this point is the essential one, imagery only begins to play this complementary role in thinking when the subject has developed operational thinking, because, without this development, the child's use of imagery is bound to lead to error and distortion, being the outcome merely of accommodation rather than of an assimilation of accommodatory activity to cognitive schemes. In fact, although we have talked of "figurative knowledge", strictly speaking this is a misnomer for we only come to know more by relating perceptions and images of objects to operational schemes. This is evident in the experiments on conservation of quantity, in which children are asked to say whether there is the same amount of liquid in Glass B after seeing it poured from Glass A, where Glass B is, say, shorter and wider than A. If in this sort of experiment the Glass B is covered and children are asked to indicate where the water comes up to, then a definite sequence of replies is observed. At first, the child believes the level in the wider glass is the same as in the narrower comparison beaker (A) and also fails to achieve conservation. Later children are successful in the anticipation of levels, but do not attain conservation, and finally they are successful at both parts of the task. Since subjects in the second category are quite able to anticipate levels but unhesitatingly set the levels visually at the same height when they are asked to estimate equality (although one glass is fatter), it may be inferred that the more or less correct imaginal representation does not lead them to an operational compensation of the type "narrower X higher = same quantity". Thus the image is limited to representing a rule such as "when a glass is wider, the water reaches a lower level" and does not encompass the causal relation that constitutes conservation; the image embodies at best a description of relationships and not a comprehension of them. However, if we take the case of subjects in the second category — those who were able to predict level but did not admit conservation — they had capitalized upon past experience, so that if imagery does not lead necessarily on to conservation, it nevertheless fixes in memory an observation which will be useful to operational thinking.

Just as accommodation in the period between two and four years of age results in imitative imagery which can only embody static representations of events, and not transformations of reality states, so assimilation is also incomplete because events are incorporated into existing schemes which are themselves not altered fundamentally by the transactions with the environment. Thus, the essential characteristic of the child's first representations is a fluctuation between egocentric assimilation, as when, for example, in playing the child utilizes an object to fulfil a particular function irrespective of the real properties of the object, and the incomplete accommodation of the imitative image. Piaget (1951) refers to these first representations as *preconcepts*. Here is a typical observation:

"OBS. 108. J. at 3; 2 (23) could not understand that Lausanne was 'all the houses together' because for her it was her grandmother's house 'Le Crêt' that was '*the Lausanne house*'. For instance, talking about a lizard climbing up the wall she said: '*It's climbing up the Lausanne house*'. The next day I wanted to see if my explanation had been understood. 'What is Lausanne? — *It's all these houses* (pointing to all the houses around). *All these houses are Le Crêt* — What's Le Crêt? — *It's granny's house, it's Lausanne*' " (p. 225).

Quite clearly, the child does not think of her granny's house as one part of a whole, the town of Lausanne; rather there seems to be both an identification of the house with a town *and* a dissociation of them. And this is typical of the pre-concept: there is a lack of true individuality of the parts of the whole and a lack of the true class concept, the idea of a whole consisting of individual parts. The emergence of a true understanding of individual identity presupposes an understanding of classification and inclusion and the emergence of an understanding of the concept of a class presupposes a grasp of individual elements. Putting this another way, we can say that the preconcept utilizes an image ("granny's house") to signify a general category (all that is referred to by the name "Lausanne") and the resulting representation is neither a general accommodation nor an accurate assimilation of the particular.

Thus, there are a number of interlocking developments in the first few years of life which are essential for the development of the ability to organize reality through the use of concepts. The development of the sense of the identity of objects, the differentiation between the subject's actions and the objects upon which he acts, the development of language that enables the subject to name and identify objects, and the development of both accommodatory activity in the forms of imitative imagery, which permits the representation and fixing in memory of reality states, and assimilatory activity in the form of symbolic play, through which the subject comes to interpret the different aspects of reality in accordance with his existing schemes. But precisely how these developments do interact is largely unknown. For example, it seems likely that the development of language owes something to the achievement of sensori-motor intelligence, but that in the course of development language itself acquires the positive function of aiding the differentiation of subjective desires from objective reality. But questions like this await further research. What we can be sure of is that all these achievements of the preconceptual period, although necessary for the formation of concepts, are not sufficient, for concept formation in the true sense of the term requires the utilization of operations which can control for the distortions produced by assimilation without corresponding accommodation, or accommodation without the necessary assimilation. It is thus to operational development that we now turn.

CHAPTER 6

The Development of Concepts
in Childhood and Adolescence

We have seen that, although the young child is capable of recognizing the permanence of objects, of applying rules of relation (as, for instance, when he says in the conservation problem that the liquid is higher because the tube is narrower), and of using words to refer to particular aspects of his experience, he is not yet capable of using concepts, in the full sense of the term, to guide his thinking and organize his world. This is because his thinking is insufficiently flexible to compensate for the distortions produced by the imitative accommodations of imagery or the symbolic assimilations of play. Both the development of imagery and the emergence of symbolic play are necessary stages in the development of concept formation, because they represent the two complementary poles of this process, the accommodation to reality and the development of a system of subjective meanings. As Piaget has argued, these two aspects of behaviour become synchronized through the child's increasing capacity to employ logical operations and it is these which ensure the establishment of stable coordinations between specific accommodations to reality and subjective interpretations. One way of characterizing operations, although by no means an adequate definition of them, is to say that they are actions that have been internalized. Through using overt actions, actual objects are related and organized; through using internalized actions, we act upon the representations of objects and thus come to understand the various transformations to which they may be submitted. The achievements and the limitations of the preconceptual phase represent, therefore, to a great extent the successes and problems of action, organized at the overt level, becoming organized internally as a system of operations. Thus, although the sensori-motor infant shows the ability to relate actions to objects, to use the same action on a variety of objects, and so forth, and these activities may be described as demonstrating the abilities of relating and classifying on this level, these abilities are not transferred immediately to the representative level and it is only gradually that pre-concepts are replaced by genuine concepts which show the same structural characteristics as these sensori-motor processes.

The most important characteristic of a flexible system of thinking is reversibility. The ability of thought to return to its starting-point is the achievement which distinguishes pre-conceptual from conceptual thinking, since for the first time, the child becomes capable of representing in a consistent manner and through an agreed name an organization of experience in which the individual parts and the whole are at once distinguished and co-ordinated. For a mode of thinking which has the property of reversibility has achieved the necessary means for correcting distortions in representation produced either by an imbalance of accommodation or assimilation. At about the age of six or seven the child is capable of using, although not perfectly efficiently from the start, two main kinds of logical operation, *classification* and *seriation*. To understand classification is to understand the relation of sub-categories to the wholes that contain them; for example, tables and chairs, beds and dressing-tables are sub-categories of the larger class of furniture. When the child has begun to think in terms of classes and their sub-classes, this means that he is able to *add* sub-classes together to produce larger classes and to *subtract* sub-classes from a class to produce an alternative classification (for example, boys = children − girls). This is an example of reversibility applied to classes and it is called *negation*. When it is applied to seriation it is called *reciprocity*. Two forms of seriation are identified, symmetrical and asymmetrical relations. In a symmetrical relationship A is in the same relationship to B as B is to A, as when, for example, A and B are "brothers". But suppose that A is taller than B, who is taller than C. Here we have an asymmetrical relationship, $A > B > C$, in which the reciprocal of "A is taller than B" is "B is less tall than A", or $B < A$. Note that a reversible transformation leaves some feature constant. Thus, the displacements of objects towards the end of the sensori-motor level do not change the properties of the object that is moved, and this is an indication of the first type of conservation − the notion of the permanent object. Similarly, at the operational level, negation and reciprocity leave the child's concept of the object unchanged, so that it may now be said that conceptual objects are conserved.

The Development of Classification

There are two major methods by which the child's ability to classify objects may be studied. The first is to present the child with a large number of objects of various kinds (or pictures of these objects) and ask him to put together those that are alike or similar. By observing how the child spontaneously classifies objects, we may infer something about the criteria that he is using and his typical mode of thinking. The second method consists of presenting the child with class-inclusion problems, asking him to judge the relationship between various sub-classes and the class that contains them. Through this method it is possible to understand how far the child has grasped the logical operations of classification. The evidence demonstrates that these two lines of study afford certain generalizations about the development of classification.

Vygotsky's work on concept formation

One of the earliest explorations of children's classifications was Vygotsky's study of object sorting, published in Russian in 1934 (Vygotsky, 1962). The test consists of 22 wooden blocks of five different colours, six different shapes of cross section, two different heights, and two different cross-sectional areas. On the underside of each block and unseen by the subject is written one of four nonsense syllables. Regardless of colour or shape, LAG is written on all tall, large figures; BIK on all flat, large figures; MUR on tall, small ones; and CEV on flat, small ones. The subject's task is to classify the blocks into four groups according to the criterial attributes of cross-sectional area and height. The nonsense syllables are used as "names" for the "concepts" involved in the four groups. The experimenter begins by turning over one block to reveal the nonsense syllable and asks the subject to select all the blocks which he thinks might go with it. The experimenter then turns over one of the wrongly selected blocks to show that it has a different name, and the subject classifies the objects again in the light of this new information. This process is repeated until the subject has solved the problem or it is evident that he cannot.

Vygotsky distinguished three age-related stages of classificatory behaviour. At the first stage, that of *syncretic grouping*, children do not achieve any kind of classification: the blocks are grouped either randomly or according to such criteria as contiguity. He called the next stage "thinking in *complexes*". Here the child does achieve classifications of the blocks in terms of their concrete characteristics, for example, by linking combinations of colour and shape, but the child does not achieve the logical classification which would enable him to solve the problem. This comes about at the third stage, in which the child is able to think in *concepts*. Vygotsky distinguished between what he called "potential concepts", which abstract only a single attribute of the blocks, and true concepts by which the subject classifies consistently according to the two criterial attributes. His description of the stages involved in performance on this task have, in the main, been validated by subsequent workers (Hanfmann and Kasanin, 1937; Semeonoff and Trist, 1958; Haslam, 1966; Stones and Heslop, 1968). The study of Stones and Heslop, in which the test was administered to a group of English children between the ages of 6 and 11, is of particular interest, partly because these authors also administered a number of extension tests which differed from the blocks in all particulars except the two criterial attributes of height and cross-sectional area, for instance, four plasticine men, a short fat man, a short thin man, a tall thin man, and a tall fat man. These tests were given after the grouping test had been completed and the child's task was to classify the figures as LAG, BIK, MUR or CEV. Stones and Heslop found a negative correlation between operating at phase one, syncretic grouping, and performance on the extension tests. They argue that this negative correlation suggests that sorting at the first level is not random, for random sorting would have produced a zero correlation between the Vygotsky and the extension tests. They conclude that children at this level are grouping according to contiguity or spatial organization which operates counter to true classification, thus producing a negative correlation.

Bruner's studies of classification

Bruner, Olver and Greenfield (1966) report two studies of the development of classification, one which used verbal stimuli and the other pictures of objects. In the first study subjects between the ages of 6 and 19 were presented with the names of various common objects and asked to indicate how they were alike and how they differed. Thus, the words "banana" and "peach" were presented and the subject asked: "How are banana and peach alike?" Then a third word, "potato", is added, the experimenter first asking how the potato is different from the banana and the peach and, subsequently, how they are all alike. This procedure was followed until 8 items had been presented.

The authors examined the subjects' classifications from the point of view of the characteristics of the object used or how the subject related these characteristics to himself and, secondly, from the point of view of the logical complexity of the rules used in classifying. According to the former method of analysis, 5 main modes of classification were distinguished:

1. *Perceptible*: The child renders the items equivalent on the basis of immediate phenomenal qualities such as colour or size.

2. *Functional*: Equivalence is based upon the use or function of the items, the subject considering either what they do or what can be done with them. Thus, a radio and a train may be put together because they both make a noise, or the radio and a light-bulb because you can turn both of them on.

3. *Affective*: The subject renders the items equivalent on the basis of the emotions they arouse, for example, "I like them" or "they are important".

4. *Nominal*: The subject groups the items by assigning to them a name that exists ready-made in the language — "they are all fruit", etc.

5. *Fiat equivalence*: A judgment which merely states that the items are alike without giving any further information, for example, "they are the same thing really".

From this point of view, the chief findings are that the 6 year olds group more often according to the perceptual properties of objects than older children; more than a quarter of their groupings are of this type and no older group forms even half as many on this basis. From 6 onwards there is a steady increase in functionally-based equivalence — from 49 per cent of all responses at age 6 to 73 per cent at age 19. The authors speculate that one of the functions of this functionalism is that it enables the child to break away from the perceptual domination of his thinking since classification by action may be used instead of classification by perceptual features.

Bruner, Olver and Greenfield distinguish three general structures in their subjects' classifications:

1. *Superordinate groupings* are constructed on the basis of a common feature or features characterizing the items in a class; thus banana, peach and potato "all have skins", etc.

2. *Complexive structures* are formed by using attributes of an array so as to form local rather than universal rules for grouping. Five kinds of complexive grouping were noted:

(a) Collections; a collection consists of finding complementary or somehow contrasting properties that the items have but without any attempt to relate the items together in terms of attributes that are shared, for example, "newspaper you can read, book you can read, telephone you can get messages over, radio you can get messages over, and a horn you can blow".

(b) Edge matchings; the edge-matching complex is formed through associative links between neighbouring items, so that a chain of items is constructed as the child ties the items together in linked pairs, for example, "banana and peach are both yellow, peach and potato are round, potato and meat are served together", etc.

(c) Key rings; the key-ring complex consists in taking an item and linking all the others to it by choosing attributes that form relations between the central item and each of the others, for example, "germs are in a banana, peach, potato, milk, water and air".

(d) Associations; in an associative complex the child links two or more items and then uses the bond between these items as a nucleus for the addition of other items; one child, for instance, having linked bell, horn, telephone and radio by the fact that "they all make noises", added the item, newspaper, on the grounds that if "you fold back a newspaper, it will crackle and make a noise".

(e) Multiple groupings; several sub-groups are formed by the subject referring explicitly to shared attributes.

3. *Thematic groupings* are formed on the basis of how the items fit into a sentence or story. One subject said: "The little boy was eating a banana on the way to the store to buy some peaches and potatoes".

At the age of 6, half of the classifications made are complexive and half superordinate, but by the age of 9 three-quarters are superordinate and by 19 the complexive grouping has virtually disappeared. If the attributes used in grouping are perceptible, then the grouping is likely to be complexive; if the attributes are functional, the chances are greater that they will be grouped in a superordinate manner. Bruner found that, when subjects are asked to group pictures of objects, there is a greater use of perceptible attributes and a lesser use of functional attributes at all ages. Nevertheless, the 6 year olds still base far more of their groupings on the way things look than do older children, and the use of perceptible attributes declines steadily. In the picture task, the use of functional attributes does not show the same dramatic increase with age that it did in the verbal task. Rather, growth takes the form of a greater tendency to use nominal classifications. Bruner concludes that classification for children aged 6 is based upon imagery, but from this point onwards linguistic structures increasingly guide classification; these linguistic structures may be used functionally (to describe what things do) or nominally (when they provide a ready-made generalization).

Kagan's studies of classification

Kagan's analyses of the development of classification have been based upon the Conceptual Style Test, which consists of a set of thirty cards, each containing three black-and-white drawings of familiar objects (Kagan *et al.*, 1964). The child's task for each of the cards is to pick out two pictures that are alike or which go together in some way and to state the basis for his grouping. According to Kagan this test measures two main types of classification and a third to a lesser extent. *Analytic concepts* are defined as involving pairings based upon similarity in an objective attribute that is a differentiated part of the total stimulus. Examples include "the watch and ruler have numbers", "the house and the pipe have smoke coming out", and "two animals have their tongues out". This type of response seems to be the equivalent of Bruner's perceptible classification. The second main type of classification measured by the test is that of the *relational concept*, which involves pairings based upon a functional relationship between two stimuli (for example, "the man wears the watch"; "the matches light the pipe") and bears an obvious similarity to Bruner's functional classification. Lastly, *inferential concepts* include pairings based on similarity in some inferred (rather than immediately given) quality and pairs involving a conventional name. This category corresponds to Bruner's nominal grouping.

In view of the apparent agreement between Bruner's and Kagan's models of classification, it is somewhat surprising that Kagan found analytic concepts to increase between the ages of 5 and 12 whereas Bruner, it will be remembered, found perceptible classifications to decrease. One possible explanation for this discrepancy lies in the nature of the two tests. Whereas the items in Bruner's tests differ from one another in all their features (i.e. they are different objects), the items used by Kagan typically differ from one another in their specific details. The analytic concept depends, therefore, upon a detailed analysis of the objects, the perceptible classification upon a more global comparison. This suggests that we should summarize these two sets of data by saying that children's classifications develop, not to become independent of perceptual attributes, but from global to analytic types of response.

In subsequent work Kagan has argued for the existence of a dimension of individual differences in reflection-impulsivity and in visual analytic ability (Kagan, 1971). He has measured reflection-impulsivity by a number of tests, including the Hidden Figures Test which requires the subject to discover a figure hidden in a complex background: impulsive children produce initially incorrect answers whilst reflective children inhibit these. Visual analysis has been measured by having children learn to attach nonsense syllables to various geometric designs. Kagan has found these two dimensions to be relatively independent of one another and of verbal ability but both contribute to performance on the Conceptual Style Test. In the light of these findings he offered the following interpretation of the attainment of analytic concepts. The most obvious way to pair stimuli on the Conceptual Style Test is on the basis of a thematic or functional relationship: the dominant association to the watch, man and ruler is a functional linking of the watch and the man or the ruler and the man, and so forth. If the child is to produce an analytic concept, he must suppress these initially strong associations and reflect over alternative responses. If, in addition to a reflective attitude, he also has a disposition for visual analysis, he is likely to produce an analytic concept. In line with this reasoning, analytic concepts, visual analysis scores, and indices of reflectivity each display a linear increase with age during the school years. However, in spite of this developmental trend, adults differ in these respects, so that we may talk of them as being measures of individual differences in styles of cognition.

Piaget's studies of spontaneous classification

In *The Early Growth of Logic in the Child* Inhelder and Piaget (1964) report a series of studies with objects and geometrical shapes for classification. The authors distinguish three general stages.

1. *Figural collections*: The child of between 2½ and 5 years of age can group objects in terms of similarities but he constantly changes his criteria of organization, being influenced first by one characteristic, then another, with the result that no general classification is attained. The end-result is best described as a collection and, since the child's responses are influenced by the figural properties of the objects, Piaget and Inhelder refer to this sorting as a figural collection. Here is an example of this kind of behaviour:

"VIV (2;6) looks first at the blue circle, then the red, and then the yellow, while saying: 'The same as that' (successive similarities). She then constructs a row of circles, ignoring the other shapes. She is asked what goes with the yellow triangle: she points to the yellow circle and then to the blue square (which also has corners). She then places the triangle and the square in a small vertical line. Finally, she arranges a series of squares in a line (also vertical), saying, 'a tower' (flat on the table)" (Inhelder and Piaget, 1964, pp. 21–2).

The change of criterion observed in such collections signifies that the child is unable to co-ordinate relations of similarity with part—whole relations. He cannot develop a scheme which "is sufficiently differentiated to comprehend all the elements of a class simultaneously" (p. 23), so that he produces a series of groupings and not a whole which includes certain sub-groups. For in order to produce a genuine classification the child must co-ordinate class *intension* (the qualities which together define membership of a class) and class *extension* (the total number of objects which possess these qualities), but the child at this stage may group objects together by similarity when he begins to order them, subsequently to fall into the error of including other objects in the grouping which do not possess the characteristic he used initially.

2. *Nonfigural collections*: From about 5 to 7 years of age there occurs an intermediate stage in which children understand many aspects of genuine classification without possessing the concept in a completely logical manner. Inhelder and Piaget list ten characteristics of true classification:

(a) There are no isolated elements; all objects are classified even if only in a class which contains one item.

(b) There are no isolated classes, i.e., every class having a specific characteristic (a) implies another class which is its complement characterized by its not having the property (a).

(c) A class A includes all the individuals having the property (a).

(d) A class A includes only individuals having the property (a).

(e) All classes of the same rank are disjoint: $A \times A' = 0$ or $An \times Am = 0$.

(f) A complementary class A' has its own characteristics a_x which are not possessed by its complement A.

(g) A class A (or A') is included in every higher ranking class which contains all its elements, starting with the next highest, B; thus $A = B - A' = B - A$: for example, if A was the class of apples and A' the class of fruit (B) other than apples, then apples = all fruit with the exception of all fruit that is not apples.

(h) Extensional simplicity: the inclusions in (g) are reduced to the minimum compatible with the intensional properties.

(i) Intensional simplicity: similar criteria (for example, colour, size, etc.) distinguish classes of the same rank.

(j) Symmetrical subdivision: if a class B1 is subdivided into A1 and A1' and the same criterion is applicable to B2, then B2 must likewise be subdivided into A2 and A2'.

Inhelder and Piaget maintain that none of these properties is universally present at stage 1, at which children do not succeed in classifying all the elements of the array or miss some out of their groups. But at stage 2 children do understand the need to class all the elements which they are given (a); they divide them into two collections or more (b); each of these contains all the elements of a kind (c) and no others (d); there is often partial complementarity (b and f) and collections of the same rank are disjoint (e); also there may be an attempt to find simplifications (h and i) and symmetries. Thus what distinguishes the non-graphic collections of stage 2 from classification in the strict sense is the fact that there are no class-inclusions (g). Consider the behaviour of the child who classifies squares (B) and circles (B') separately; then he proceeds to divide the squares B into red ones (A) and blue ones (A'), and next does the same with the circles. It certainly looks as though this child were applying properties (a) to (j), but we would not be justified in this conclusion without further inquiry. For a distinction must be made between the subdivision of collections and the subdivision of classes in the strict sense. In a genuine classification the subject understands that A and A' are contained in the next higher class B; he knows therefore that daisies and tulips are included in the class of flowers, tables and chairs within the class of furniture, and so forth. The larger class B conserves its identity as a class with certain sub-classes even when those sub-classes are dissociated in time or in space because the subject understands the relation of class inclusion (A = B − A'), i.e. the daisies are the flowers minus the tulips. But compare this understanding with the behaviour of a child at stage 2 in the development of classification:

"CLA (7;0). Like BAC, first juxtaposition and then reduction: two cars, an engine and two prams 'because they all roll'; two horses, two owls and two chickens 'because they're all animals'. If you wanted to write what there is inside, what word would you use? — 'Six animals'. . . . Are there more animals or more chickens? — 'More animals, because . . . no! more chickens!' — Why? — 'Because there are three birds (forgetting an owl), yes, that one too' (i.e., four) — Then are there more chickens or more animals? — 'More chickens' " (Inhelder and Piaget, 1964, pp. 57—8).

3. *Classifications*: Just as it is an error to believe that a very young child has the concept of a class simply because he can say that a daisy is a flower or a lady is a person, so it would also be false to conclude that the child's difficulties in classification are resolved at the period of concrete operations at about 7 years when he becomes capable of grasping the relation of class-inclusion in certain cases, for example, flowers or geometrical designs. Inhelder and Piaget give examples of children over the age who do not yet appreciate the logical properties of classification with certain kinds of material. For example, when asked to classify spontaneously various animals, children of this age are more inclined to classify in terms of familiar properties, such as "wild—tame" or "animals that fly" and "animals that walk", rather than abstract verbal categories. Consequently, the subjects are often unable to achieve completely integrated classifications, as, for instance, when one child begins with a class of insects, but goes on to put ducks with the mice ("fairly small animals"), and the birds with the frogs. Because the level of reasoning varies with the concrete character of the material, this stage is known as the concrete operational period. "Unless the objects fall easily into a nesting set of classes each of which is

readily distinguishable by virtue of an obvious perceptual criterion, the classification breaks down" (p. 114). It is only from about 11 or 12 years onwards, that there is a formal or abstract understanding of classification:

"TRA (12;4) begins by putting the ducks and frogs in A, the birds and bats in A', and the insects and other animals in B'. But he decides to start again, putting the insects in A, after first removing the spider, the birds and bats in A' (so that A + A' = 'animals that fly'), and the other animals in B'. 'Are there more insects or more flying animals?' — More flying animals because the insects are all flying animals — 'More flying animals or more animals?' — More animals because those that fly are still animals — More flying animals or more birds? — More flying animals, because there are birds and insects" (Inhelder and Piaget, p. 116).

This work demonstrates that, although children can detect similarities between objects from an early age and group objects on this basis, the development of an understanding of classes takes place over a number of years and is attained most completely only when the child has grasped the logical operations involved in class inclusion. A concept, it has been asserted, is a stable organization of experience which is brought about through the application of a rule of relation and to which is assigned a particular name. One of the most important results of Piaget and Inhelder's work is the demonstration that this stability of experience is not something "given" in perception but the outcome of a sequence of development in the use of logical operations. As their results with classes and sub-classes show, the young child is quite capable of understanding that tulips and daisies are flowers but not capable of understanding that this operation (A + A' = B) is logically equivalent to its inverse (A = B − A'), in which the daisies are a sub-class of a whole which contains it and other sub-classes. For, when the young child argues that there are more daisies than flowers, he fails to conserve the whole (B) and to understand that A is quantitatively less than B. And when class inclusion is understood, it is limited at first to objects which are perceptually discriminable and only gradually develops into an abstract understanding of the principle of classification.

One further point needs to be made about the development of the concept of classification. The traditional theory of abstraction, it will be recalled, relied heavily upon the notion that the formation of concepts occurs as a result of the perception and classification of similarities among objects. We understand now, however, that to classify objects is not simply to attend to their similarities, because the development of classification involves in the first place an assimilation of reality to the subject's point of view and secondly the development of logical operations which enable the subject to overcome the distortions produced by his focussing upon one aspect of the situation to the neglect of others. This means that the development of what are usually called "simple" or "everyday" concepts is inextricably bound up with the development of logical concepts, of which the concept of classification is the most important since it permits an understanding of the world of objects and their relationships in a class. But there are other developments in logical thinking taking place from early childhood to adolescence and it is to these that we must now turn.

The Development of Seriation

In forming a classification, objects are ordered by their similarities and the differences between them set aside. In the seriation of objects, on the other hand, the subject's task is to order the items along one or more dimensions according to the differences between them. Piaget (1952) reports a number of studies designed to investigate the development of seriation and of serial correspondence. He asked whether it was easier for the child to construct a single series of objects arranged along one dimension, for example, size, or to construct two corresponding series, for example, dolls and balls varying in size. The former appears to be the simpler task, for the second series might just be a complication to the child. Or it could be that the child is helped in the construction of a series by their being a correspondence between the items of that series and another. In fact, he found that the two are parallel developments. At the first stage, children are typically both unable to form series and to construct corresponding series. They are unable to order a set of dolls by their size because they cannot bear in mind that each element has got to be both larger than the preceding ones and smaller than those that follow. Consequently, although they can understand the idea of something being "larger than" or "smaller than" something else, children at this stage tend to deal with the individual objects in succession and fail to achieve a coherent series. Similarly, when the child is asked to put a series of dolls opposite a series of balls also differing in size, his efforts meet with only partial success. These results are due, Piaget suggests, to the fact that all correspondence presupposes seriation and when spontaneous seriation is not possible, neither is serial correspondence, and vice versa. At the second stage the child overcomes these limitations: he is capable of spontaneous construction of a series after a certain amount of trial and error and can successfully solve the problem of serial correspondence, usually by first making a series with one set of objects, making a separate series with the other, and then making each item in the first series correspond with the item having the same position in the second series. But the child's understanding is not fully operational, a fact which is not immediately apparent but requires further exploration from the experimenter. For instance, a child at this level is incapable of inserting new elements into a series in the correct positions. And he cannot find corresponding items when one series is bunched together or reversed. These limitations are overcome at the third stage, at which the child forms the series, not by trial and error, but by the application of a definite rule such that at each step he looks for the biggest (or the smallest) of the remaining elements. Now the child no longer hesitates in judging the two series to be equal in number when the order of one is inverted or the series is displaced.

"BOS (6;6), Question II: Whose is this ball (B8)? — (He pointed to D8.) — How do you know? — I can see 3 there (B10, 9 and 8) and there (D10, 9 and 8). — And this one (B6)? — It belongs to that one (D6) because there were 3 and now it's jumped to 6 (so he had counted balls 1—6). — What did we do? — Before, there were 3 (10, 9, 8) and now we've jumped to 5 (this time counting balls 10, 9, 8, 7, 6 and dolls 10—6 and again pointing to D6 and B6)" (Piaget, 1952, pp. 113—4).

The Development of the Concept of Number

One of the major implications of Piaget's work on concept formation is that great care must be taken in the attribution of understanding in the child for an apparent skill in the use of concepts may mask crucial limitations in the child's thinking. This generalization is nowhere more in evidence than in the field of number and mathematical conceptualization. That the child can recognize that there are more objects in one pile than in another or that he has learned to count objects set before him does not necessarily signify that the child understands the operations involved in elementary mathematical relations. For saying that there is "more" in one heap than in another may well be a perceptual (not an operational) estimation, and counting apples may be for the young child an exercise in rote learning (and not an understanding of relations). To trace the development of mathematical understanding, then, is to trace the development of those logical operations which are at the basis of addition, subtraction, and so forth.

In particular, Piaget holds that the construction of whole numbers occurs in close connection with the development of class inclusion and seriation, and that, consequently, the same stages are evident in the three areas. In order that the child should understand numbers, he must grasp the principles of class inclusion *and* seriation because a number is at once a member of a class and a member of a series. Recall that to assign an item to a class involves treating items within a class as identical with respect to the class criterion and ignoring differences between items. Now this is just what we do when counting the number of apples or beads: each item is treated as being equivalent to every other and differences in the concrete characteristics of the items are set aside. But, although the units of whole numbers are identical, the numbers form into a series which is asymmetrical: $8>7>6$ or $3<4<5$. Thus numbers have the peculiar characteristic that they are both elements within a class, and in this respect are all equivalent, and also elements within an asymmetrical series, in which respect they are all different. Number is a synthesis of inclusion and seriation.

We have already examined some of the difficulties of the young child in the use of class inclusion and seriation and the stages involved in overcoming these limitations. However, it would be a misrepresentation of Piaget's views to suppose that number develops out of these operations and is the result of them alone. This is because there are certain differences between numbers and classes. With numerical units the parts are homogeneous units, but the parts of a class are still only qualified classes which are united through certain common properties. Therefore, although in both class inclusion and number there is the addition of parts to produce a whole, adding one item of a class to another in the same class does not produce a change in the class but adding one number to another does, since a new number is produced. Therefore, it is necessary to carry out certain experiments to determine whether the child understands these peculiar characteristics of number. Does he understand, for example, the additive composition of numbers, that is, the fact that different numbers may be added together to produce the same result (4 + 4 = 1 + 7)? Piaget (1952) tested this by telling the child that he is to have four sweets for "elevenses" and four at tea-time on one day but one sweet in the morning and all the others in the afternoon on another day, and demonstrated the numbers involved in these statements by dividing 8 beans in the appropriate manner. The child is asked to compare the two lots, 4 + 4 and 1 + 7, and to say whether he will eat the same number on both days. Once more, we find three stages, one at which the two sets are not regarded as equivalent, a third at which they are, and an intermediate stage. Another set of experiments investigated the child's understanding of "multiplicative composition", presenting the subject with three series, say, two kinds of flower and a number of vases, and showed that it is only at a third stage, that of concrete operations, that the child has a firm grasp of "two-to-one" relationships, for example, two flowers for each vase, or, if another set of flowers is produced, three per vase, and so forth.

The Development of Conservation

Undoubtedly the concept which has been most thoroughly investigated is that of conservation. The experiment on conservation of substance using variously shaped containers is well known (Fig. 6.1). The pre-operational child believes that when the liquid in glass B is transferred to glass C there is no longer "the same" amount as in A, although he had granted that there was initially the same amount in glass A and glass B. This conservation is attained at about the age of seven, the conservation of weight at about two years later, and that of volume, measured as the amount of water displaced by the immersion of an object, at approximately the age of eleven.

One manner of describing the failure of the young child on these tasks is to say that he characteristically focuses his attention upon one dimension only and is therefore unable to co-ordinate the changes that occur

Concept Formation

Fig. 6.1. *A procedure for assessing the conservation of liquids*

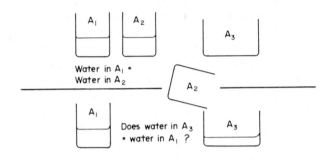

Source: from M. Manis, *An Introduction to Cognitive Psychology*.

along two dimensions. Thus, he might state that glass C contains less than glass A since the level of the liquid is not as high, or he may say there is more because class C is "fatter". Piaget argues that the child has to learn to decentre his attention in order to understand that the decrease in height is compensated for by the increase in width. He calls the argument for compensation reversibility by reciprocal relationship in distinction from reversibility by inversion in the case in which the child admits conservation "because the water can be poured back" (into B). Both these arguments signify an understanding of the logical operations involved in true conservation and thus mark the beginnings of concrete operational thinking which is able to deal adequately with the transformations of objects (classification, seriation, conservation) and is not restricted to judgments of states of objects. However, there has been considerable controversy over the meaning of conservation responses and one of the major complications in this area has been the fact that a child can grant conservation although he may not have reached the stage of concrete operations. This is because it is possible for the child to admit conservation through an appeal to the

identity of the material: "it is the same water" (Bruner *et al.*, 1966). Piaget
(1968) maintains that this is a "pseudo-conservation" and that it is necessary for the examiner to inquire further of the child to determine whether
he has advanced to an operational understanding of conservation.

The Development of Abstract Concepts

As conceptual development continues, the child is able to make increasingly efficient use of abstract concepts. We have seen that the idea of
"mummy" and other early notions is intimately related to the child's own
activities and desires to begin with, both Werner (1948) and Piaget in his
early work (1926, 1928) pointing to the animistic character of early thinking. Similarly, with respect to the development of logical and mathematical
thinking, the child may be said to possess the concepts in his action, that is
as he manipulates concrete objects, but he does not possess logical concepts
as objects of thought, that is, as well-defined operations, of which he is
explicitly aware. Thus, the concrete-operational child knows how to classify
objects and relate them in an asymmetrical series but he is unable to treat
his own activities of classifying and seriating as the material for further
operational manipulations. The development of the capacity to operate
upon operations is the characteristic of abstract thinking. An integral part
of this capacity is the development of an understanding of hypotheses
because a subject who has objectified his own activities as elements of
thought can now regard these activities as *possible* ways of ordering and
interpreting objects and events, that is, as hypotheses that may be confirmed or not. It is true that the child before the age of eleven or twelve
has a sense of the possible, since the very asking of a question presupposes
an implicit belief that alternative answers are available, and there is some
sense in regarding any concept as the means whereby the subject predicts
the likely course of events. But it would be false to call the thinking of the
pre-adolescent child "hypothetical" on these grounds, for to be able to
entertain an hypothesis is to be able to reflect upon one's own ideas and
test evidence systematically against them. Finally, abstract thinking implies
the ability to combine possibilities systematically; just as the child succeeded
in classifying objects, so the adolescent succeeds in understanding the need
to work through all possible combinations in order to test his hypotheses.

The difference between the thinking of the child and of the adolescent is apparent when these subjects are given problems which have to be worked out mentally rather than with the aid of materials. Thus, as we have seen, the concrete operational child demonstrates an understanding of transitivity in ordering dolls or balls of different size, but he is unable to solve problems of transitivity when asked to seriate representations of objects. In his early study of judgment and reasoning in the child, Piaget (1928), administered some tests devised by Burt involving transitivity. For example, the child was asked: "Edith is fairer than Susan; Edith is darker than Lily. Who is the darkest, Edith, Susan, or Lily?" Children who failed this task either saw a contradiction in the test (how can Edith be both the darkest and the fairest?) or put Edith in the middle of the three, saying that Lily is the darkest and Susan the fairest. This is because they tended to identify "darker than" with "darkest" and "fairer than" with "fairest", that is, they thought in absolute rather than relational terms, although such tests require only those operations which the children had successfully used with concrete materials. Here we have an example of the need for logical concepts to become independent of particular situations in order to be truly general.

From this point onwards the subject becomes increasingly able to reason with propositions. Inhelder and Piaget (1958) report a series of experiments designed to investigate the growing capacity for propositional reasoning. Subjects were asked to discover such facts as the laws governing the oscillation of a pendulum, the correct combination of chemicals to produce a yellow mixture, and the laws governing the size of a shadow projected on to a screen using the materials depicted in Fig. 6.2. The subject is asked to find two shadows which cover each other exactly, using two unequal rings. To achieve this end he needs to place the larger one further from the light, in proportion to its size, for this will result in compensation between distances and diameters. The concrete operational child does understand the compensatory relationship of distance and size, but he tends to think of distance as the distance between the rings and the screen, rather than the distance between the light source and the screen, and he thinks in terms of additive relationships rather than multiplicative ones. The adolescent, on the other hand, is capable of understanding the inverse, metrical proportionality which exists between the distances from the light source and the diameters of the rings, and eventually may arrive

Fig. 6.2. The projection of shadows

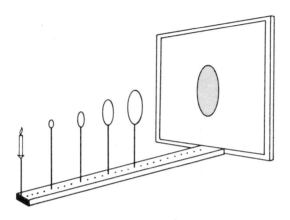

The apparatus involves a baseboard, a screen attached to one end of this, a light source, and four rings of varying diameters. The light source and the rings can be moved along the baseboard. The subject is asked to produce two shadows of the same size, using different-sized rings.

Source: from B. Inhelder and J. Piaget, *The Growth of Logical Thinking.*

at the general rule that the distances have to have the same relation to each other as the rings, i.e., the ratio has to be the same. We may say that the child then possesses the concept of proportionality. It should be noted, however, that there is some controversy over the question as to whether abstract logical and mathematical concepts such as these are found in most adolescents and adults or whether their incidence is dependent upon social and educational opportunities (Parsons, 1960; Smedslund, 1963; Lunzer, 1968). It must be remembered that Piaget's concern is to describe the highest achievements of which thought is capable at different stages of development rather than to supply normative data on the development of concepts. He would certainly maintain that the performance of adolescents on abstract reasoning tasks is dependent upon the utilization of logical operations connecting propositions, but would agree that it is doubtful whether subjects are aware of the operations they use if they have not received formal training in logic.

Evidence from other studies confirms that abstract concepts develop only in later childhood and adolescence. Sturt (1925) concluded that a child begins to acquire an understanding of time concepts related to the study of history at about 10 years of age. Friedman (1944) found that the idea of a "year" was not properly grasped until the age of 9 and that only about two-thirds of 12-year-olds understand words like "recent", "eternal", and "B.C.". When asked to state what differences there are between the past and the future, children under the age of 11 tend to provide a simple definition of the form, "the past is before the future" or "the past has happened, the future has yet to occur", whilst children over this age include abstract characterizations of the difference; examples of such characterizations are: "we look forward to the future, but back on the past"; "mistakes can be made in the future, but we cannot make mistakes in the past", and "the future is dependent upon the past, but the past is not dependent upon the future" (J. Cohen, 1967).

Piaget (1932) and Kohlberg (1971) have described the emergence of more abstract moral concepts in adolescence. For Piaget, one of the most significant transitions in moral development is the development from judging the worth of actions by their objective consequences to judging them according to the intentions of the agent. For Kohlberg, moral development proceeds from a *pre-conventional level*, in which the individual is sensitive only to the pleasant or unpleasant consequences of his actions, through a *conventional level*, in which morality is regarded largely as conformity to social expectations, to a *post-conventional level*, which at its highest point involves reference.to principles of justice and mutual respect which are held to be universally valid and binding. He presents evidence to support his view that this progression is observable in all cultures, except that some cultures do not attain the higher levels and, within a culture that does, the morality of the highest stages will often exist alongside conventional morality, rather than totally replacing it. The theories of Piaget and Kohlberg are "cognitive-developmental theories", suggesting how conceptual development in the social and moral field occurs in parallel with general conceptual development.

In the same manner, it has been observed that the ways in which children describe other people change from the concrete to the abstract (Watts, 1944; Brierley, 1966; Livesley and Bromley, 1973). At first, children describe others in terms of external and physical attributes, but from the age of 7 increasing reference is made to psychological qualities and the child becomes increasingly skilled at reconciling apparently contradictory qualities through his increasing ability to make inferences about behaviour. Livesley and Bromley maintain that these changes are largely a consequence of the child relinquishing an egocentric attitude and developing operational modes of thinking:

> "As he becomes capable of inferential thought, he integrates events separated in time and finds underlying regularities, similarities and consistencies in the other person's behaviour. He thus forms a concept of the other person which is not dominated by the immediate and concrete stimulus situation" (p. 148).

Inhelder and Piaget (1958) maintain that just as the pre-operational child is egocentric, since he is unable to decentre his attention from his own perspective to the perspectives of others, so at the initial phase of abstract thinking, concepts are invested with personal overtones and become the instruments of grandiose schemes for altering reality. It is difficult to assess the truth of this idea. On the one hand, it has been supposed that adolescence is a time of crisis and role-diffusion (Erikson, 1950), and this notion fits in with the fact that a sense of the possible is acquired at this age, but it would perhaps be a mistake to characterize this period as one of intellectual and emotional storm and stress. Douvan and Adelson (1966), summarizing their study of American adolescents, conclude that on the whole their subjects are not deeply involved in ideology, nor prepared to do much thinking on value issues of any generality. Instead, the authors argue, most adolescents adopt defences which result in the curtailment of experience and the limitation of self-development and differentiation. It seems, therefore, that although the capacity for abstract thinking develops from adolescence onwards, it is with respect to only certain problems, especially those in which subjects receive formal tuition, that the flexibility of thinking, which the use of abstract concepts may foster, becomes evident. In addition, it is probable that the adult's conceptual behaviour ranges between the concrete and the abstract use of concepts and that some of our concepts remain at a level which is intuitive and action-bound.

This last point raises the general question of the role of experience in the development of concepts. We have so far restricted our consideration of conceptual development to description of the order of attainment of types of concept. There does, indeed, seem to be a considerable amount of agreement among investigators about the general sequence in which concepts are formed. But this should not be taken to mean that this order is entirely the result of maturational factors or that different cultures develop the same concepts in the same order. We must now turn, therefore, to the question of the mechanisms responsible for the learning of concepts.

CHAPTER 7

Concept Learning in Childhood and Adolescence

This chapter is concerned with research into the ways in which concepts are formed during childhood and adolescence. It is restricted to this age range since there is a recognizable body of work on children's concept formation that is quite distinct from both studies of concept formation in adults and studies of concept attainment. These topics are considered in subsequent chapters. Concept learning in children has been extensively investigated, but, in contrast to the study of the sequence in which concepts develop, there remains considerable controversy over the question of how this process should be characterized. In particular, there are a number of opinions about the relative roles of associative and structured learning in concept formation and about the complementary problem of whether the motivation for cognitive development is to be found by reference to the principles of reinforcement or by reference to cognitive drives. A third and by no means subsidiary issue concerns the medium in which thinking progresses: this is the question of the roles of language, action, and imagery in concept learning.

Associative and Structured Learning

In discussing the traditional theory of abstraction, we concluded that the doctrine of associationism is powerless to explain the formation of concepts because a concept, however primitive, is always a particular organization of experience. The rudimentary concepts that Freud talked of as occurring in dreams are not random associations but images organized through wish-fulfilment; the first concepts of the child — pre-concepts and collections — are organized according to themes of action or desire. But, it may be argued, there is surely an associative aspect to experience; we learn a concept in specific circumstances and incorporate features which are not, strictly speaking, an essential part of the concept: they just happen to be there. For example, Kagan (1964) has shown that young children tend to think of school as typically feminine. He taught 6 and 7 year old children to associate three different nonsense syllables with masculine objects (a tie for example), feminine objects (a dress for example), and agricultural objects (haystack, etc.). After they had learned to sort the pictures, they were asked to classify others which included school-related items, such as a blackboard and a page of arithmetic, as well as some further, "neutral" agricultural items. Kagan's results suggested that young children tend to view common objects in the classroom as more closely associated with femininity than masculinity and this is probably due to the fact that they are taught mainly by women and perhaps because they engage in such "feminine" pursuits as singing, dancing and painting. Now this sort of learning appears to be best described as associative. Masculinity/femininity is not an essential aspect of the definition of the concept of school but, nevertheless, it is an important part of these children's concept of school.

No one would wish to deny that there are such associations in our use of concepts, both in childhood and adulthood. But the interesting question from the point of view of a psychological theory of concept learning is to determine how such experiences may be incorporated in a general explanation. With respect to this goal, a number of solutions have been proposed. Some theorists, especially those within the S—R tradition, regard associative learning or conditioning as the major, if not the only, form of learning; others have suggested that there are *types* of learning, some more advanced than others, and that associative learning occurs at an early stage in development but is superseded by structured or cognitive learning; and at the opposite extreme to the first group are those theorists who argue that all learning is, in some sense, organized and who, therefore, see little room for mere associations. Before considering the views of each of these schools, let us be as clear as possible about the issues involved. In particular, we must be careful to define exactly what we mean by "learning a concept" and make sure that we are not oscillating between different uses of the expression to suit our own convenience.

For example, Thorndike's experiments with the cats in the puzzle-box are often quoted as examples of "trial-and-error learning", "problem-solving", or "thinking". But, as Collingwood (1940) has pointed out, there is a vast difference between Thorndike's description of the animals' activity and the ways in which human adults use trial-and-error in solving problems. Thorndike's animals escaped the box in the course of random movements as they scratched and clawed at the front of the box. But this is not what we normally intend by the expression trial-and-error. Rather, a process of deliberate experimentation is signified in which the person frames a hypothesis, observes its consequences, and adjusts his behaviour accordingly. Thus, although there is some merit in attempting to reduce complex behaviour to processes considered to be more basic or simple, this end will not be achieved by using a term, which is properly used with reference to certain kinds of behaviour, to refer to other kinds of behaviour which are quite different in nature. The two previous chapters have demonstrated different levels of conceptual functioning, so that the question that must be asked now is: what is the role of associative learning at each of these levels?

Associationist Theories of Concept Learning

The modern version of associationism states that a subject learns a concept through a process of conditioning. If a subject is presented with several displays of stimuli which differ in some respects but are similar or identical in others, he will associate these common elements or resemblances with a particular response. Thus, the child perceives a great many different types of building but learns to associate the word "house" with only one particular class of them. The application of well-formed concepts to less familiar situations may be explained by taking into account the number of features the situations have in common. Harlow (1959) has argued that the subject has to experience a variety of examples of a particular concept before the concept is formed. On his view, a concept is a learning set developed in the course of the subject learning to respond correctly to varying examples of the concept. He has shown how monkeys can learn always to choose squares, rather than other shapes, even though the squares differ in size, or how they can learn to respond to the odd stimulus, when presented with groups of three stimuli, two of which are alike.

One of the limitations of this view, which is recognized by theorists who wish to remain within the S—R tradition, is that it is not possible to point to identical stimulus elements or perceptual similarities for many concepts; for example, dominoes, ice-hockey, and swimming may be classified as "games" but what stimuli do they have in common? An associationist theory can be extended to include such instances by arguing that, when there are not discernible resemblances among stimuli, the learning process is one of association alone, the connection between stimulus and response being formed through contiguity. In this way, it is thought, we learn to group together such articles as hats, ties, and shoes under the heading of "clothing": there are no identical elements or similar perceptual relations, so that the concept can only be learned through the association of the same word with the different objects. But, in extending the associationist theory in this way, it may be acknowledged that there is at least one important difference between concept learning in animals and in human subjects, namely, that humans possess words which act as mediators between the stimulus and the overt response and that, therefore, they are able to form concepts and to change them in response to different circumstances much more rapidly than animals.

This line of reasoning has been advanced by Kendler and Kendler (1962). They maintain that two theories are necessary to explain concept learning, a single unit S—R theory to account for the behaviour of animals and children who cannot make use of symbolic mediation, and a mediational S—R theory for older children and adult subjects. This conclusion was reached through the analyses carried out by the Kendlers and their associates on reversal shift behaviour. Let us look at an early experiment in detail which illustrates the two major kinds of conceptual shifts that have been studied. In an experiment by Kendler and D'Amato (1955), in which college students acted as subjects, two stimulus cards were used: a large, orange diamond, and a small, dark-grey ellipse with pointed ends. There was a deck of 32 response cards which varied in terms of four forms (circle, crescent, square, and a [-shaped figure), four colours (black, grey, yellow, red), and two sizes. The two major concepts that the subjects were required to respond to in this experiment were shape (S) and colour (C). The learning of the shape concept required that rectilinear shapes (the squares and the [-shaped figures) be sorted below the large, orange diamond, and curvilinear shapes (circles and crescents) be sorted below the small, grey ellipse. The colour concept required that the subject place the achromatic figures below the small, grey ellipse and chromatic figures below the large, orange diamond.

The experimental procedure also included the learning of a reverse shape (RS) and a reverse colour (RC) concept. These reverse concepts required the subject to sort the cards in a manner opposite to that of the "direct" concept. For example, in the learning of the RC concept, the subject has to learn to sort the achromatic response cards below the large orange diamond, and chromatic response cards beneath the small grey ellipse. The learning of the reverse of the original concept is called a *reversal shift*. A *non-reversal shift* consists of the subject shifting to learn the previously irrelevant dimension.

The main purpose of the Kendler and D'Amato experiment was to compare the relative effectiveness of a reversal shift as compared with a non-reversal shift. There were four groups of subjects: S—RS, S—RC, C—RS, and C—RC. They sorted the cards beneath the two stimulus cards and were told after each case whether they had made the correct choice or not. The transition between the two stages of the experiment is made without informing subjects of the changes in criteria.

The investigators predicted that their subjects should execute reversal shifts more rapidly than non-reversal shifts. An account of the theory responsible for this prediction is given by Kendler and Kendler (1962). The S—R theory applicable to adult behaviour on the concept shift problem is one which assumes that between the external stimulus and the overt response there occurs a mediational mechanism, so that the external stimulus evokes an implicit response which produces an implicit cue that is connected with the overt response, or S—(r—s)—R, instead of S—R. The Kendlers assume that these implicit stimulus and response events observe the same principles that operate in observable S—R relationships, that is, principles of conditioning, and they present a schematic diagram of the different predictions of single unit S—R theory and mediational S—R theory (Fig. 7.1). According to single unit theory the non-reversal shift should occur more rapidly, because at the time of the shift the difference between the strength of the dominant incorrect habit and the to-be-correct habit is much greater for the reversal than the non-reversal shift. That is, having established the concept of responding, say, to chromatic objects by placing them under the orange diamond, the strength of this habit will

Concept Formation

Fig. 7.1. *Predictions from S—R and mediational theory concerning reversal shift behaviour (from Kendler and Kendler (1962))*

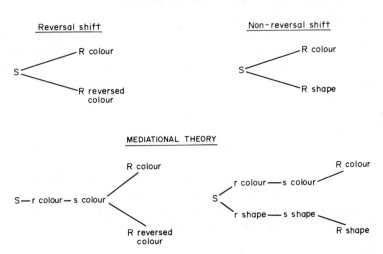

interfere more with the learning of the reverse concept than it will with the learning of a new S—R connection. However, according to mediational theory the situation is quite different. A reversal shift enables the subject to utilize the same mediated response and only the overt response has to be changed, whilst a non-reversal shift requires the acquisition of a new mediated response, the cues of which have to be attached to a new overt response. Thus, because the old mediational sequence has to be abandoned and a new one formed, the non-reversal shift should be executed more slowly than a reversal shift.

The experiment by Kendler and D'Amato confirmed that adult subjects learn reversal shifts more rapidly than non-reversal shifts. Other studies produce similar results and also show, on the whole, that animals (rats, pigeons, rhesus monkeys) execute non-reversal shifts more quickly than reversal shifts. The Kendlers carried out experiments to determine the age at which human subjects change from finding non-reversal shifts easier to finding reversal shifts easier. They found that this change seems to occur at about 6 years of age and they believe that the mediational processes which children over this age can utilize in concept learning are probably verbal in nature. It is the implicit or explicit labelling of the relevant and irrelevant stimulus dimensions in the concept shift task which makes for the relative superiority of reversal over non-reversal responding.

As reviews of the literature indicate (Wolff, 1967; Slamecka, 1968; Bolton, 1972), there is considerable disagreement over the existence of a transition from non-reversal to reversal responding in children and whether verbal mediation is implicated in this transition. The evidence from studies which provide verbal training in order to facilitate reversal responding is, at best, equivocal, and this stands in contrast to the evidence from studies which have utilized training directed at allowing the subject to gain insight into the organization of the stimuli. Tighe (1965) advances the view that it is increased sensitivity to the stimulus variables themselves which plays an important role in promoting the dimensional control of discriminative responses which is assumed to be necessary for rapid reversal. According to this viewpoint, organisms differ, both individually and developmentally, in their ability to detect stimulus dimensions and to utilize such invariant properties of stimulation in concept learning. These differences are assumed to stem from differences in the organism's opportunities, learning ability and perceptual experience. Tighe tested this idea by giving 5- and 6-year-olds non-reinforced pre-training designed to emphasize the independence and the dimensional nature of the properties used in the subsequent discrimination experiments. His experimental group was asked to match stimuli differing on two dimensions with a standard stimulus; the control group had to make up a story around some pictures. He found that this pre-training facilitated the performance of the reversal shift but did not affect the performance of the non-reversal shift. Tighe suggests that this facilitation resulted from an improvement during pre-training in the subject's ability to detect and utilize the distinguishing features of the stimuli. The nature of the pre-training errors indicates that the most difficult judgment was one which required the subject to use variations in a single dimension to specify differences (i.e., discrimination); most of the pre-training improvement involved this ability. Such results have been obtained in other investigations (Tighe and Tighe, 1968, 1969). Of particular interest are studies by Johnson and White (1967) and White and Johnson (1968). These authors interpreted Tighe's findings to suggest that training children to perceive particular stimulus values as ordered points along a dimension facilitates reversal shift performance. Going a step further, they argued that the concept of dimensionality underlies reversal responding. Therefore, they administered a test of the child's understanding of dimensionality — a seriation test which required stimuli varying in size or brightness to be ordered along the correct dimension. It was found that subjects who made fewer errors on the dimensionality test made fewer errors on the reversal problem and understanding of dimensional relations was correlated with tendency to execute reversal shifts more rapidly than non-reversal shifts. These experiments, therefore, support the hypothesis that reversal shift behaviour involves increased attention to perceptual cues rather than the utilization of mediational processes.

The principal argument against the associationist theory of concept learning is a logical one: we can and do distinguish between associations of ideas and concepts which organize ideas. But it is apparent that the empirical evidence also weighs against the theory: organization at the perceptual or at the conceptual level is implicated by studies which train subjects at concept shift problems.

Theories of Types of Learning

Alternative conceptions of concept learning accept the criticism that associationism cannot account for higher-order concepts which depend upon principles of organization, but retain associations as one type of learning, usually the most basic. Such a view is put forward by White (1965) in an article which reviews evidence on developmental changes in intellectual functioning in childhood. There is, indeed, impressive evidence that the age range 6–7 years is an important turning-point in intellectual development. We have already observed that, according to Piaget, the transition to concrete operational thinking occurs at this age, and, according to the Kendlers, that reversal shifts become relatively easier than non-reversal shifts from this age onwards. Factor analyses of intellectual tests also reveal changes in modes of functioning (Hofstaetter, 1954), it becomes more difficult to condition children after they have reached this age (Razran, 1933), and they find moderate degrees of complexity in stimuli more pleasing than extremes of simplicity or complexity (as adults do) — Munsinger *et al.* (1964). White comes to the conclusion, therefore, that at this point in development an associative mode of responding is being replaced by a cognitive mode. He draws a parallel with Freud's (1915) distinction between primary and secondary processes; thinking governed by the primary process is said to follow the "pleasure principle", for associations between ideas occur through wish-fulfilment, whereas the secondary process obeys the "reality principle" and thinking is rational and adaptive. Just as Freud believed that the young child had access only to primary process thinking, so White argues the initial, associative mode of responding must be inhibited to give way to the cognitive level. He believes that this transition is a continuous and gradual process.

A similar dichotomy has been proposed more recently by Jensen (1969). He talks of Level I and Level II ability. Level I ability is defined as the capacity to register, store and recall stimuli without any transformation or organization of these stimuli taking place: the subject does not have to "do" anything with respect to the stimuli; he has simply to record as faithfully as possible, as, for instance, in rote learning tasks. On the other hand, Level II ability is characterized by organization of the input and we test this ability in traditional intelligence tests and in tests of concept formation. Jensen proposes that the two sets of abilities follow different courses of development that are related to socio-economic status. Level I abilities are seen as developing rapidly within the first seven or eight years of life and having the same course of development and final level in both lower and middle socio-economic groups, whilst Level II abilities develop slowly at first, show a spurt between four and eight years of age, and show an increasing difference between social class groups.

All these schemes have in common the theme that the young child responds in an associative manner, the older child in an organized way. The apparent virtue of such ideas is that the lower levels of functioning provide a base for the development of higher functions, as, for example, in Gagné's (1970) scheme. Now, no one would wish to deny that there are qualitative differences in the ways in which children of different ages learn and we are in agreement with Jensen and Gagné in wishing to reserve concept learning for higher developmental levels. But I believe that it is incorrect to view associative learning as an ability or as a concept which adequately describes the learning of young children or infants. If a concept is always an expression of a particular organization of reality, then the association of a stimulus with a response is not, for the subject, part of his use of a concept, although it may well be for the experimenter who is teaching the subject the concept in an associationist manner. Forming an association is failing to learn the concept, for concept learning can only be described as the process whereby one comes to distinguish between those elements which are an essential part of the concept and those which are not. How, therefore, can a period of associative learning lead to a period of concept formation? The plain and simple answer is that it cannot, and that if we examine the course of intellectual development we find the child's behaviour to be normally guided by cognitive structures from the level of the reflex upwards. In short, as we saw in the two previous chapters, true concepts are the outcome of a developmental sequence whose stages differ in kinds of organization, rather than there being two levels, at one of which behaviour is organized and at the other it is not. It is thus to cognitive theory that we now turn.

Cognitive Theory of Concept Learning

Piaget's theory has been criticized on a number of occasions (Bandura and Walters, 1965) for failing to specify precisely enough the mechanisms responsible for the child advancing from one stage of development to the next. It is asserted that Piaget might provide us with a comprehensive description of development but the absence of a detailed theory of learning means that he does not provide us with an adequate explanation of development. But this criticism is an oversimplification, for Piaget's theory of intellectual development does contain an explanation of the process of learning, namely, the equilibration process. Recall that to attain conservation the child has to understand how the increase along one dimension is compensated for by a decrease along the other, or how the action of pouring the liquid into the comparison beaker can be reversed and the water poured back into the standard container. One way of explaining nonconservation is to say that the child's attention focuses upon one aspect of the situation to the neglect of the other, and that he is able to admit conservation when he "decentres" his attention. Piaget (1957) has proposed a probabilistic model of conservation learning which illustrates the equilibration process. The general thesis is that focusing upon one dimension increases the probability of attention switching to the other, presumably through habituation and contrast, so that eventually the child oscillates between, say, asserting that there is "more liquid" in the comparison beaker, because it is taller, and asserting that there is less, because it is narrower. The child is thus led to recognize the problem and the error of his previous judgment; he is now motivated to use logical operations of reversibility and compensation to justify a conservation judgment. Piaget believes that intellectual development as a whole is governed by equilibration, which may be defined in general terms as the tendency for development to advance to more stable forms of adaptation: the changes in intellectual development from the sensori-motor level through the pre-operational and concrete operational level to formal reasoning are characterized in terms of the stability of the cognitive structures at each stage: the logical operations of formal thinking are more abstract and hence more stable than concrete operational structures which are linked to specific aspects of the environment, but these in turn are more stable than pre-operational modes of thinking. The concept of equilibration has been criticized by Bruner (1959) on the grounds that it is not precise enough to specify the ways in which thinking becomes adapted to particular environmental circumstances. Whilst it is true that the principle is a general one, some notion of cognitive conflict appears essential to any theory of intellectual development, witness Hunt's (1961) idea of an optimal "match" between the child's capacities and environmental stimuli, or Bruner, Olver and Greenfield's (1966) theory of conservation being the result of a conflict between alternative means of representing reality.

Smedslund (1961a,b) was the first investigator to present evidence in favour of the cognitive conflict hypothesis of conservation attainment. He believed that it is cognitive conflict itself, rather than feedback about the correctness or incorrectness of his response, that induces the child to acknowledge conservation. Accordingly, his training procedure aimed to provoke conflict without knowledge of results. Children between the ages of 5½ and 6½ years who were non-conservers of quantity were subject to a training procedure in which the deformation of the object (a ball of plasticine) was simultaneously opposed by some addition to, or subtraction from the object; for example, if a subject believed that the elongation of a ball of plasticine made it "more" than one initially judged to be equivalent, the experimenter would subtract a piece from the elongated plasticine, hoping to induce a conflict for the child between saying that there is more because it is longer and saying there is less because some has been taken away. Smedslund found that such techniques led some non-conservers to admit conservation on a post-test and to support their judgments with logical arguments. These studies, therefore, provide some support for the notion that equilibration is important for the development of conservation and Smedslund contrasted these limited but positive findings with the failure of other methods, for example, those relying upon external reinforcement.

The work of Bruner and his colleagues (reported in Bruner, Olver and Greenfield, 1966) may be viewed as an extension of Piaget's ideas about the equilibration process. The thesis elaborated by Bruner is that there are three major ways in which reality may be represented. It may be represented enactively as, for example, when the sensori-motor child comes to know more about the properties of his environment through his acting upon it; or it may be represented ikonically, that is, through the medium of imagery; or it may be represented symbolically, that is, through the medium of language which Bruner sees, as Piaget does, as arising from a general symbolic function, defined as the capacity to let one object "stand for" or represent another. Although, also, the two theorists are in agreement that these three modes of representation show a developmental sequence from the enactive through the ikonic to the symbolic, Bruner believes that Piaget neglects the role of imagery in cognitive development and the fact that these forms of representation are available to the person at any time and that it is the conflict between them which promotes cognitive growth. An experiment that was carried out to test these ideas had to do with the conservation of quantity and children were asked to judge whether a ball of clay which assumed a different shape was the same as another which did not change but which had initially been judged to contain the same amount. The experiment involved four main forms of training and eight conditions. Training in inversion involved a reversal of the transformed piece of clay to its original shape; this was either carried out by the child himself ("manipulation") or by the experimenter ("no manipulation"); training in compensation involved the use of verbal labels (such as "thicker", "thinner") as the reversal to the initial state occurred, again with and without manipulation; and there was also a choice between screening and not screening the alterations made upon the material, for in an earlier experiment on the conservation of liquids it had been found that placing a screen between the child and the objects during their transformation is effective in fostering conservation based upon an appeal to the identity of the object, i.e., it is the same object. In this experiment, Bruner argued that screening would have the effect of preventing the child from relying upon a misleading ikonic representation and forcing him to rely upon other forms of representation. In fact, screening was found to have virtually no effect on conservation learning, inversion was relatively ineffective, but manipulation and labelling (compensation) were effective *together* in promoting learning, although neither one by itself was so. These results were interpreted along the lines that manipulation and labelling encouraged the use of modes of representation (enactive and symbolic) which came into conflict with the dominant ikonic mode; that the enactive or the symbolic mode alone conflicts with the ikonic is evidently not enough; it is only when the two combine against the ikonic that the child can be liberated from his dependence upon misleading perceptual cues.

A great deal of research has been carried out into the problem of how the child acquires conservation, however, and the cognitive conflict hypothesis is just one of the explanations put forward. As reviews of the literature make clear, no one explanation commands unequivocal support (Lunzer, 1968; Sigel and Hooper, 1968) and it has become increasingly apparent that several factors have to be taken into account. Other than the child's increasing competence in the use of logical arguments, there are developments in linguistic competence which have a bearing upon the conservation problem (Cohen, G. M., 1967; Lumsden and Poteat, 1968), for children have to learn how to use words like "same" and "more" correctly; others (Gelman, 1969) have argued that the child has to learn not to attend to misleading perceptual cues in order to grant conservation; or, as Bryant (1971) has suggested, it may be that the child understands the equality of the two standard beakers in conservation of liquid, he understands that the transformed liquid is the same as that in the beaker, from which it was poured, but is unable to *remember* the perceptual data and thus fails to make the transitive inference that the transformed liquid is the same amount as that in the standard beaker. The task which faces future research is to determine by analyses which will have to be both painstaking and original just how such variables interact, for it seems very likely that in dealing with perceptual development, the development of operational competence, memory, and language, we are confronted neither with processes which are completely independent of one another nor with processes which are completely dependent upon one another but with something "in between" these two extremes. Making explicit just what this "in between" means is probably the most serious challenge that research into concept learning has to meet.

There are promising indications that research workers are becoming more aware of this problem. This is illustrated in the findings of Inhelder and Sinclair (1969), Strauss and Langer (1970), Inhelder, Sinclair and ·Bovet (1975) and Youniss (1971) who show that there is an interaction between learning and developmental level. As Youniss points out, Piaget sees development, as manifested in available operational schemes, as itself a determinant of learning and not just a process which can be reduced to particular learning experiences. For example, subjects who are in the transitional stage for, say, conservation or class inclusion, show the most marked improvement as a result of training, whilst those in the stage below tend not to alter their judgments as a result of training. We can perhaps generalize from these results to suggest that concept learning occurs under those conditions in which there can be a productive interaction between the existing repertoire of cognitive skills (operational, linguistic, etc.) and specific experiences which "match" the properties of the repertoire, at least in some respects. Several authors have argued for the idea that development progresses through there being an optimum level of dissonance or uncertainty in the interaction of the person and his environment: Berlyne (1960) refers to this principle to account for exploratory behaviour, Thomas, Chess and Birch (1968) in order to account for the development of a personality that can cope with changing circumstances. The task of arranging environmental conditions in order to promote optimum growth of concept formation is the central problem for a theory of instruction; Chapter 10 reviews work in this area. There is the further problem of individual differences in the transformation of information from the environment; for example, some subjects may prefer less uncertainty than others or they may categorize more broadly; Chapter 9 offers an account of what we know about such differences in response style which clearly need to be taken into account by any theory of learning or instruction.

In Summary

The associationist viewpoint has persisted in the form of S—R learning theory either in a pure variety, which recognizes no other form of learning than conditioning, or in a "mixed" theory, which assigns the doctrine of association to a lower developmental level, although, nevertheless, a fundamental one. Of more recent origin in psychology are cognitive explanations of concept learning which suggest that in the learning of a concept it is the activity of fitting new elements into existing modes of organization which is crucial, rather than merely associating these elements through reinforcement or contiguity. Thus, whatever differences there are between the theoretical positions of Bruner and Piaget, they would both agree that to learn a concept is to have either a tacit or an explicit understanding of a rule whereby stimuli can be organized and that, consequently, it makes sense to ask whether the subject's knowledge of the concept is genuine or to what extent it contains features that are present because the subject has failed to discriminate the essential from the inessential aspects of the concept. A central feature of this perspective is that intrinsic motivation is the prime determinant of cognitive growth; it is some conflict between the subject's expectancies and his observations, especially, one supposes, observations of changes brought about by his own activities, which promotes concept formation, rather than reinforcement itself. And, finally, it is argued that it is not a question of reducing concept learning to one mechanism or to one particular ability, such as language or memory, but of understanding how developments in a number of abilities interact and mutually influence one another whilst remaining at the same time discriminable aspects of the same general process of concept learning. But we have only just begun to investigate this problem.

It must be emphasized, however, that supporting a cognitive theory of concept learning does not amount to a total rejection of the efficacy of associative learning or of external reinforcement. Peters (1958), in discussing the concept of motivation, has suggested that there is no one, all-embracing explanation of motivation; rather, there are a number of types of explanation, such as explanations of motivation as rule-following behaviour or explanations which deal with situations in which a person feels under some compulsion to do something. If to learn a concept is to learn a rule by which elements may be related, then it is clear that types of explanation which have nothing to say about the process by which rules are understood, that is, associationism or conditioning, are not appropriate forms of explanation for concept learning. But they may well be appropriate forms of explanation for behaviour which is not guided by rules, that is, for the irrational behaviour of the organism which has no insight into the situation and which, consequently, performs in a panic or haphazardly, like Thorndike's cats, or in a rote, mechanical way, like Skinner's pigeons. And, moreover, there may well be associative aspects to many, if not most, of a person's concepts: Kagan's young subjects *associated* school with females rather than *learned the relationship* between the categories of males and females and the category, school. However, to take this kind of learning as a paradigm for concept learning leads to the absurdity that one is no longer in a position to distinguish between behaviour which represents a genuine understanding of reality and behaviour which does not.

CHAPTER 8

Concept Formation in Adult Subjects

Concept Formation and Attainment

Bruner, Goodnow and Austin (1956) proposed that a distinction should be drawn between concept formation and concept attainment. The former refers to the process of establishing a new category, whilst the latter refers to the activity of discovering which elements belong to the category and which do not. These authors take as their paradigm for concept attainment the behaviour of the gourmet who wishes to discriminate between edible and non-edible mushrooms. He already knows that two such classes exist but is not yet sure of the attributes which enable him to distinguish between them. Thus, "attainment refers to the process of finding predictive defining attributes that distinguish exemplars from nonexemplars of the class one seeks to discriminate" (p. 22). If, on the other hand, the subject's task was to sort mushrooms into some meaningful set of classes through establishing categories which would organize them in some way, then we should talk of concept formation. Therefore, according to Bruner *et al.*, in order for the task of concept attainment to begin the subject must have already formed some concept, and in this sense it may be said that concept formation is the more fundamental process.

However, we may question the psychological reality of the distinction between concept formation and attainment. If to form a concept is to identify stimuli as instances of a type, as was suggested in Chapter 2, then what Bruner calls concept attainment is really concept formation and there is no justification for supposing two distinct psychological processes. For in both "attainment" and "formation" the subject's task is to determine the attributes that serve to identify stimuli as instances of a type. This is the activity involved in defining mushrooms and in defining edible mushrooms: the attributes that define the classes differ in these two cases but the psychological process is essentially the same. Wetherick (1976) has developed this viewpoint.

What Bruner, Goodnow and Austin achieved, therefore, was a very good working definition of concept formation and the significance of their work was that thinking need no longer be regarded as a covert process that escapes the reach of empirical investigation. In the studies reviewed in this chapter, subjects are required to learn the defining attributes of positive instances of a concept as these are specified by the experimenter.

Bruner, Goodnow and Austin's summary of the essential aspects of this task is succinct and bears repetition:

1. There is an array of *instances* of the concept. These instances vary in terms of their *attributes*, for example, colour, weight, and in terms of attribute *values*, the particular colour or weight.

2. After each instance the subject *decides* whether or not the instance is a member of the category or not.

3. The subject attempts to *validate* his decision through finding out whether his choice was correct or incorrect or indeterminate.

4. Each decision and test provides potential *information* by limiting the number of attributes and attribute values which are to be considered in the future.

5. The sequence of decisions made by the subject during concept attainment may be regarded as a *strategy* embodying certain objectives: (a) to maximize the information gained from each decision and test of an instance; (b) to keep the cognitive strain involved in the task within manageable proportions, and (c) to regulate the risk of failing to attain the concept within a specified time.

This framework for the study of concept attainment has proved influential and many, more recent, formulations are strikingly similar to it. Let us now look in more detail at the nature of the task used by Bruner and his associates and then consider his characterization of the task more fully.

The material for the task consisted of a deck of 81 cards, which varied in shape of figure depicted, number of figures, colour of figure, and number of borders around the figure. The subject is told that the experimenter has a concept in mind such as "all red cards" or "all cards containing red squares and two borders", that certain cards that will be presented to him are illustrative of the concept while certain other cards also presented are not, and that it is his task to discover what the concept is. The experimenter begins by showing the subject a card that illustrates the concept, a positive instance. The experiment continues in this fashion, the subject being told after each card whether his categorization of the card as belonging to the concept or not was the correct one. The subject is required to attain the concept as efficiently as possible. It may be noted that this procedure corresponds closely with Bruner's characterization of the process of concept attainment, according to which the subject has to decide on the basis of observed instances which attributes define the concept and each decision amounts to a prediction whose outcome provides potential information related to future choices.

In describing the sequence of decisions made by subjects, Bruner, Goodnow and Austin were able to isolate a small number of strategies. The strategy of *simultaneous scanning* involves the person using each instance in order to deduce which of his remaining hypotheses are still tenable and which have been eliminated. Since the subject's aim is to consider all possible eventualities within a deductive framework a great load is placed upon memory and reasoning capacity. For example, if the subject has narrowed the concepts down to three, red cards, circles, or red circles, he has to choose whether to test for one of the single attributes or the two together; he might think that if the concept were in fact "red circle" and he chose to test red and circle, the discovery of a positive instance does not eliminate either of the other two alternatives. This choice would, therefore, be mistaken. But logically there are nine possible outcomes to consider (three choices against three possible correct solutions) and the elaboration of this table proves too much for the majority of subjects. A more defensible strategy is that of *successive scanning*, in which the subject tests a single hypothesis at a time, that is, for example, he follows up the hypothesis that the concept is "red" until he encounters a negative instance. The cognitive strain imposed by this strategy is minimal but a lot of information may be lost during the sequence of decisions since the person is only focussing upon what is directly relevant and once an hypothesis is invalidated he has to begin anew with another. A third strategy, which combines the merits of a more systematic approach with one involving less strain than simultaneous scanning is *conservative focussing*. This consists of finding a positive instance to use as a focus, making a series of choices, each of which alters only one attribute value of the first focus card, then testing to see whether the change results in a positive or negative instance. If the change results in a positive instance, this logically eliminates the attribute from consideration since *no* value of such an attribute can be relevant to the concept. The fourth strategy, *focus gambling*, is more risky, in that the subject uses a positive instance as a focus and then proceeds to change more than one attribute value at a time. This procedure may yield the correct concept in a very short time (if the person is lucky and the attributes which he chooses to vary simultaneously make no difference) but when a negative instance is encountered the subject has to revert to simultaneous scanning in order to discriminate between the possibilities inherent in a negative instance and eliminate hypotheses.

Whilst these strategies are described by the authors as "ideal strategies" and it may be sometimes difficult to discern the precise relationship between these and the subject's actual behaviour, the importance of this work lies in the fact that it externalized the steps involved in conceptualization. The chief technical problem in the path of the advancement of the psychology of thinking is simply that thinking is a covert activity and, if we are to understand this process, it is necessary that the subject's behaviour at different stages of a task should reflect the different components of this activity. This is the great merit of the concept attainment task of Bruner, Goodnow and Austin: concept attainment became amenable to experimental investigation. Thus, it was shown that, when permitted fewer instances in which to attain the concept, subjects tended to switch to the more risky strategy of focus gambling. But more important than such specific findings is the general implication that the factors influencing concept attainment may be understood through experimental manipulation. However, Wetherick (1976) has urged caution in generalizing from such experiments to "real life".

Bruner, Goodnow and Austin were concerned with three major types of concept, which are called *conjunctive, disjunctive,* and *relational*. A conjunctive concept is defined by the joint presence of the appropriate value of two or more attributes. Thus, "three red circles" is a conjunctive concept. For a disjunctive concept, one *or* more of the attribute values defines the category, so that cards showing circles, three figures, red circles, circles, three circles, three red figures, or three red circles would each belong in the disjunctive category. The relational concept owes its form to a specifiable relationship between defining attributes, that is, to the existence of a logical rule which the subject must grasp if he is to attain the concept. "Cards with the same number of figures" and "cards with fewer figures than borders" are relational concepts since they involve the use of logical terms such as "same" and "less than". This is not to say that relational concepts are defined by the presence of logical rules whereas conjunctive and disjunctive concepts are not, for all concepts depend upon some form of logical order, whether this is conjunctive classification or disjunctive or any other definite rule for linking elements. It is the fact that some rules are more difficult to learn than others which is responsible for a characteristic order of difficulty of types of concept, and this topic is the one to which we now turn.

Order of Difficulty of Types of Concept

Neisser and Weene (1962) investigated the relationship between a logically ordered hierarchy of concepts and difficulty of concept attainment. The simplest concept logically is defined by the presence or absence of a single attribute: a vertebrate is defined by its having a backbone, an invertebrate by not having one. At the next level of logical difficulty are concepts defined by the presence of two attributes, which are either conjoined, disjoined, or negated: in a simple conjunction of two attributes, both attributes must be present; with a disjunctive concept, either one or the other or both must be present; the relation of negation may enter into the definition of a concept in a number of ways: the concept may involve attribute A being present and attribute B absent, as for example, when the law rules that eligibility for a driving licence depends upon passing a test (A) and not being subject to epileptic fits (B); or it may be that both A and B must be negated: harmless snakes are those without poisonous venom and the habit of constricting. At a higher level still are concepts defined by rules such as "either A or B must be present, but not both together". Neisser and Weene hypothesized that concepts at higher levels of logical difficulty would be more difficult to attain than those at lower levels. They confirmed this hypothesis using strings of four consonants as stimuli and the various concepts being defined in terms of the presence or absence of one or of two of these letters. Their results indicated that the difficulty of a concept is related to its logical complexity with univariate concepts, for example, "the presence of attribute A", being the simplest, conjunctions and disjunctions of two attributes somewhat more difficult, and concepts of the form "either A or B must be present, but not both together" and "both A and B must be present, unless neither is" the most difficult.

Bourne (1970) has extended this kind of analysis. He distinguishes between attribute and rule learning. In the former, the subject is given the rule by instruction but has to learn to identify the attributes which enter into the definition of the concept; in rule learning, on the other hand, the relevant attributes are given and the subject must identify the rule which links them into a concept. The major rules for relating two attributes are illustrated in Fig. 8.1. Bourne had subjects (college students) learn a series of rule-learning problems and found that there were significant positive transfer effects between problems of the same logical form: solving one problem based upon a particular rule in general improved performance in another problem based on the same rule. He also found a considerable amount of positive transfer between problems of different logical

Fig. 8.1. Conceptual rules for binary concepts

Primary rule		Complementary rule	
Name	Verbal description	Name	Verbal description
Affirmative	all red patterns are examples of the concept	Negation	all patterns which are not red are examples
Conjunctive	all patterns which are red and square are examples	Alternative denial	all patterns which are either not red or not square are examples
Inclusive disjunctive	all patterns which are red or square or both are examples	Joint denial	all patterns which are neither red nor square are examples
Conditional	if a pattern is red then it must be a square	Exclusion	all patterns which are red and not square are examples
Biconditional	red patterns are examples if and only if they are square	Exclusive disjunctive	all patterns which are red or square but not both are examples

Source: Adapted from Bourne, 1970.

complexity and traced this to the acquisition by subjects of an understanding of the logical structure of the series of tasks. The subject acquires, not a number of rules, but a conceptual system of rules.

"He knows how to solve problems based upon any rule within the system. He has encountered and solved a series of problems exemplifying a small set of rules, and from that experience he has learned a more general conceptual system. Just as the objects are positive instances of a class concept and class concepts are positive instances of a rule, the rules can be said to be positive instances of the system" (p. 555).

This, and several other studies (Bourne and Guy, 1968; Haygood and Bourne, 1965; Neisser and Weene, 1962), confirm that the order of difficulty of concepts is from the affirmative through the conjunctive, inclusive disjunctive to the conditional. Bourne and Dominowski (1972) note that the placement of the biconditional rule in this order is uncertain, some studies indicating that it is the most difficult, while others show it to be easier than the conditional or disjunctive rule. This question deserves further study.

The Utilization of Positive and Negative Instances

A concept is learned through the subject becoming familiar with examples of it (positive instances) and of cases which fall outside the category (negative instances). There has been some debate over the relative effectiveness of positive and negative instances in concept attainment. Smoke (1933) reported that success in concept attainment was not significantly greater when subjects worked with a series of instances, half of which were positive and half negative, than when they worked with positive instances alone. He concluded that negative instances do not convey very much information to the subject about the concept. This conclusion was, however, criticized by Hovland (1952) who argued that it was not clear from Smoke's study whether negative instances are ineffective because of their low value as carriers of information or whether because of the difficulty of assimilating the information they do convey. For example, in Smoke's experiment, the syllable, "dax", was to be associated with the concept of a circle with one dot inside and one dot outside. The instances presented to the subject varied in terms of the size of the circle and the exact position of the dots. The subject was informed that the instance was positive or negative by the display of a plus or minus sign. But, Hovland points out, in the absence of a clearly formulated convention for the experiment which the subject knows about as much as the experimenter, there is no control with such an experimental procedure of the amount of information conveyed, for factors not intended by the experimenter to be relevant may be selected by the subject; for example, in Smoke's experiment a subject might think that a "dax" is a circle with one dot inside and one dot outside *on a white background*. In fact, Smoke commented that his subjects were frequently able to distinguish between correct and incorrect instances in the test series but were unable to define the concept correctly and it seems likely that this was because they had included characteristics which were considered irrelevant by the experimenter. Hovland developed a method for overcoming this problem; it involves, essentially, equating the amount of logical information conveyed by positive and negative instances. Suppose, for instance, that the concept to be attained was "white circle" (of any size), that is, there are three dimensions, each of which has two values (size: large—small; shape: circle—square; and colour: black—white). In this case, there will be two positive instances (*large white circle* and *small white circle*) and the remaining six will be negative. If only positive instances are used in the learning series, then both are required to transmit the concept, but if the series is to be made up only of negative instances, the correct solution can be attained by successive elimination of each of the six wrong instances (in fact, in this example, five negative instances will eliminate eleven of the twelve possible hypotheses the subject might have about these stimuli). The question of the relative usefulness of positive and negative instances may now be reformulated: how efficiently will the subject reach the concept when he is shown only two possible instances as compared with the situation where he is shown the five negative instances?

An answer to this question was attempted by Hovland and Weiss (1953). They found that negative instances were more difficult to utilize effectively, even when the amount of information conveyed by negative and positive instances was equated. It is thus clear that subjects do experience difficulty in using information concerning the attributes which are not in the concept to be learned. Later studies have confirmed this conclusion.

Bruner, Goodnow and Austin (1956) reported that their subjects were unable or unwilling to use information which is based upon negative instances and attributed this to a distrust of "in-the-head" transformations, that is, of reasoning. Freibergs and Tulving (1961) argued that people use positive instances more than negative instances in everyday life and that this experience transfers to experimental investigations of concept attainment. If this reasoning is correct, the superiority of positive instances should decline in an experiment in which the subject is given practice in the use of negative instances. Freibergs and Tulving found this to be the case: a group of subjects using positive instances initially performed more efficiently than a group using negative instances but, after several practice problems, the difference between the performance of the two groups almost disappeared.

As Bourne (1965) pointed out, these early studies of positive and negative instances were limited to concepts based upon unidimensional or conjunctive rules. For an instance to be positive with such concepts, it must contain all relevant attributes and this fact means that in ordinary circumstances positive instances will carry more information about a concept than negative instances; furthermore, positive instances will provide a natural focus for strategies employed to identify relevant attributes. But these advantages do not hold for disjunctive concepts which are based upon the "and/or" rule. For in a disjunctive concept a positive instance contains one or more relevant attributes, whereas a negative instance must embody no relevant attribute. Thus, disjunctive concept attainment should be easier with a series of all negative instances. This hypothesis has been confirmed by Schroth and Tamayo (1972). Such work leads to the generalization that the critical variable in relation to the difficulty of concept attainment is not the difference between positive and negative instances but the difficulty of the inferential strategy: the easier inferential strategy is associated with positive instances of conjunctive concepts but with negative instances of disjunctive concepts (Bourne and Dominowski, 1972).

Concepts as Decision Trees

There is implicit in these ideas the assumption that concept attainment consists of a series of decisions; at each stage of learning the subject must decide whether the instance presented to him is an example of the concept or is not. Thus, the difficulty of a concept is attributable, among other variables, to the length and complexity of the decision process. Hunt, Marin and Stone (1966) were among the first to suggest that concept learning may be represented as a sequence of tests of the values of individual attributes. For example, the concept of "legal driver" may be "any one who is not a felon and who has passed the driver's test". The sequence of decisions necessary to allow the subject to assign instances to this class may be represented in the form of a *decision tree*. Points at which the subject makes a decision (by answering a yes/no question) are called *nodes* and it is apparent that a concept involving fewer nodes will be easier to understand, other things being equal, than one involving many nodes. The authors analyse several different types of concept in these terms. Figure 8.2 illustrates the decision trees involved in five different types of concept. Problem 1.1 is a conjunctive problem: positive instances are those objects which have both characteristics A11 and A12. Problem 1.2 is an inclusive disjunctive problem: positive instances have either characteristic or both

Fig. 8.2. Decision trees for five kinds of concept

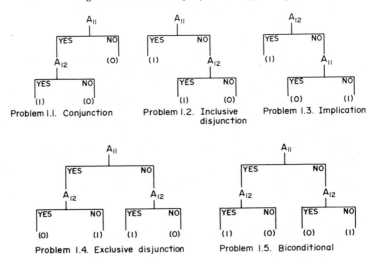

Source: from E. B. Hunt, J. Marin, and P. J. Stone, *Experiments in Induction.*

of them. Problem 1.3 involves implication for the presence of A11 implies the presence of A12 (all positive instances have characteristic A12 or do *not* have characteristic A11). Exclusive disjunction, in which all positive instances have one or the other characteristic but not both, is illustrated in 1.4, and in 1.5, the biconditional, either all positive instances have *both* characteristics or they have *neither* characteristic.

Hunt, Marin and Stone used this notion of concept identification as a sequential process to write computer programmes which could model the behaviour of human subjects. Essentially, their "concept learner" operates in the following manner. A sample of objects is selected randomly from the universe of items; the first item in the sample is transferred to the memory section of the concept learner, which then uses this stored information to compute a trial concept. The next stage consists of transferring the next item of the sample to memory, and the trial concept is now used to classify the new item. If the classification turns out to be correct, a further item is selected, if incorrect, a new trial concept is developed. This process is repeated until there are no more objects in the sample. Developing computer programmes which incorporated these features, the authors were able to show that difficulty of concept learning is related to the complexity of the decision sequence for both the concept learner programme and the human subject. In one experiment, for example, in which mean number of errors was plotted against type of concept to be learned, they found a general similarity between the performance of their human subjects and computer output, in that conjunction and inclusive disjunction were the easiest types to learn and implicational exclusive disjunction and biconditional being progressively more difficult.

More recently, Hunt (1971) has reformulated the hypothetical decision process occurring in concept attainment, taking into account the possibility that there are a number of different types of memory involved. In this Distributed Memory Model there is a long-term memory, in which information is stored permanently, and conscious memory, which contains a processing unit and two memory areas, a short-term memory, which holds a very exact picture of recently received input, and an intermediate term memory which stores a general picture of what is going on at the time. Using these concepts, Hunt reformulates the decision process as follows. The learner observes objects of known classification and a description of a particular object arrives in short-term memory. The subject's hypothesis about the class of the object exists as a decision rule in intermediate term memory and when the description of the object arrives in short-term memory the hypothesis is used to classify it. If the classification is correct, a new object is sought, but if the classification is incorrect, a new hypothesis is constructed based upon the current contents of short-term memory. In constructing the new hypothesis some use may be made of information in intermediate term memory and of information in long-term memory about the kinds of attributes that may be relevant. The programme which constructs the new hypothesis may be regarded as a concept attainment strategy similar to those discussed by Bruner, Goodnow and Austin and by Hunt, Marin, and Stone. A similar decision-tree analysis has been proposed by Trabasso, Rollins and Shaughnessy (1971), who distinguish between storage and verification stages in concept attainment. The general idea in this model is that in storage subjects represent the attributes of objects in affirmative form, whilst in verification they are set to make identity matches between particular instances and these coded representations. Both these models are, of course, hypothetical and, no doubt, further studies will be forthcoming in this area to clarify the roles of inference and retrieval from memory.

Mathematical Theory of Hypothesis Testing

Mathematical models of hypothesis testing in concept attainment are not concerned with describing the nature of the hypotheses used by subjects but with *predicting* the subjects' behaviour by *assuming* that they are testing and rejecting hypotheses. Restle (1961, 1962) has proposed such a theory, assuming that a problem stimulates a number of hypotheses, some of which are correct in so far as they lead to the problem's solution, while most of them are incorrect. Restle isolated three possible strategies in the utilization of this pool of hypotheses. In the first strategy the subject chooses at random one hypothesis from the pool which is maintained until it leads to an error; it is then returned to the pool and a new hypothesis chosen. It is evident that this refers to the successive scanning strategy of Bruner, Goodnow and Austin. In a second strategy, the subject begins by considering all the hypotheses in the pool simultaneously. After the first stimulus, a proportion of these hypotheses will suggest that it is a positive instance, another proportion that it is a negative instance; the response made by the subject is determined by the larger of these two proportions. If the response is correct, all hypotheses consistent with the contrary response are eliminated, and this process is continued until the subject finishes with one correct hypothesis. This is akin to simultaneous scanning. The third strategy is a compromise between the first two and involves the subject beginning with a *sample* of hypotheses from the pool (not just one, as in the first strategy, and not the whole pool, as in the second). But the process is again one of elimination until the correct hypothesis in the sample is attained or the sample is exhausted. Restle's theory has been found to account for many of the quantitative aspects of subjects' behaviour on simple concept attainment problems. An account of the work stimulated by the theory can be found in Van de Geer and Jaspars (1966) and in Bourne and Dominowski (1972). However, the theory makes the assumption that a subject can remember only the hypothesis or hypotheses he is currently using and that, therefore, when a hypothesis is rejected because of an error, he cannot remember those hypotheses which have been rejected on earlier trials. This seems most unlikely and illustrates the necessity of adjusting mathematical models of concept attainment to the probable psychological events underlying the quantitative predictions.

An alternative mathematical model has been elaborated by Bower and Trabasso (1964), Trabasso and Bower (1966), which proposes that there are two fundamental processes; the first process is that of stimulus selection, which consists of attending to a particular stimulus dimension or attribute. It is assumed that stimulus selection proceeds in an all-or-none fashion: before the subject attends to the relevant dimension, his probability of making errors is constant, but upon selecting the relevant dimension the probability of error is zero. The second process is that of associating a response to a particular value of the relevant dimension; it is assumed here that this conditioning takes place very rapidly in a simple concept attainment problem. As Bourne *et al.* (1971) point out, the major difference between this and Restle's theory is that it assumes that the subject has a limited memory for preceding events, for on each error trial the subject is said to make a "consistency check", comparing information given in that trial with the one preceding it. Dimensions which fail to pass this test are eliminated. This happens if the same attribute is assigned to different categories or if different attributes from the same dimension are assigned to the same category on these two trials.

Although the Bower and Trabasso model differs from the one proposed by Restle in assuming that subjects remember disconfirmed hypotheses, it shares the assumption that the subject rejects possibly relevant stimuli on the basis of these leading to error. Learning occurs, therefore, only on error trials. However, Suppes and Schlag-Rey (1965) asked subjects to classify the entire stimulus array into two categories on each trial (thereby revealing the currently held hypothesis) and found that almost as many changes occurred in classification on correct response trials as occurred on error trials. The tendency to change on correct response trials was not restricted to certain problems or subjects but was a general phenomenon. Similarly, Levine (1966) found that subjects make use of information provided by correct responses and that their category responses on any particular trial tend to be consistent with *all* previous trials. This led him to formulate a theory whose central feature is that the subject is assumed to devise a new hypothesis on each trial at the time of stimulus selection and in advance of feedback. That is, the subject takes the attributes of the stimulus first associated with positive reinforcement as a composite hypothesis and then attempts to narrow that hypothesis down as some of the attributes are found to be irrelevant. In this way the subject makes use of feedback from correct trials to eliminate some of the stimulus attributes.

Although the available evidence does not allow us to ascertain the uses and limitations of these various models, it seems likely that each is most appropriate within a particular context and that the further from this context the concept attainment task is, the weaker the theory. For example, Levine has worked with problems which are relatively simple in structure and he has given his subjects explicit instructions and a lot of practice; under these circumstances it is possible for subjects to utilize logically complex deductive strategies. The clarification of these mathematical models would probably also be aided by linking them more explicitly with theories about the psychological processes involved in such tasks. Here, the work of Hunt (1971) and of Trabasso *et al.* seems most promising. Looking back upon work in concept attainment in the last two decades, there is some justification for asserting that the insights of Bruner, Goodnow and Austin have been built upon and there is every hope of further progress towards a systematic account.

CHAPTER 9

Individual Differences in Concept Formation

Within the last few years several investigators have proposed that individuals differ in the ways in which they process information, that these are enduring features of an individual's personality, and that such differences have repercussions for cognitive functioning. Unfortunately, it is not immediately apparent what relationship these postulated dimensions have to one another, whether they in fact represent independent dimensions of cognitive style or whether there is some definite pattern of relationship between them. But, although such a basic question as this remains unanswered, it is desirable at this point in our consideration of concept formation, to discuss cognitive styles in relation to concept formation since there is a striking resemblance between these dimensions along which individuals may be ordered and the theoretical position, outlined in Chapter 3, that there are a number of stages in concept formation distinguished by the type of attention exercised. For many of these hypothetical cognitive styles have to do with attention deployment and the way seems open for a reconciliation of experimental work relating to the general process of concept formation with studies of individual differences. It is probably this lack of co-ordination between these two fields of inquiry which has played the major role in the profusion of theories about individual differences and it has as yet proved a difficult task to understand the implications of such differences for problem-solving behaviour: they have appeared as differences in style, rather than ability, and we have been confronted with the unsatisfactory position of not knowing how style and ability are to be systematically related in our explanations of cognitive functioning. The reconciliation of the theory of concept formation with work on individual differences in cognitive style is likely to be a long and arduous process. As Jensen (1966) has remarked, it is difficult enough to understand concept learning without bringing individual differences into the problem. Nevertheless, we are in a position to make a start and in this chapter I shall outline the major generalizations suggested by current work.

Perhaps the most appropriate point of departure would be to try to conceptualize the process of concept formation in the most general terms. I have argued earlier (in Chapters 1 and 2) that it is mistaken to oppose hypothesis-testing theories of concept formation to "copy theories", that is, those which assume that the subject has simply to attend to stimuli in order to recognize resemblances among them. The copy theory of concept formation is wrong because stimuli are organized from a particular point of view or with a particular intention in mind. But, equally clearly, we do pay attention to the characteristics of our environment and we are not restricted, normally, to testing hypotheses in the abstract way of the scientist: for we do have access to a fund of experience which is not directly subordinated to a definite hypothesis, experience which has been described, as we saw in Chapter 3, as occurring in the fringe or horizon of consciousness. This state of affairs may be summarized by asserting that in general our experience is compounded of both intentional and attentional aspects. To intend something is, of course, to mean a particular thing but there is implicit in every intentional process a typical form of more general alertness; similarly, to attend is to be prepared to notice things, but certain things are more likely to be registered than others because they are more consistent with the intentions underlying the act of attention. The terms, intention and attention, are being used here in precisely the way in which Piaget uses the concepts of assimilation and accommodation. We can say, either: every adaptive act involves both assimilation to existing cognitive structures and accommodation of those structures to the new experiences; or, every advance in concept formation involves both the exercise of an intention and an act of attention. Adaptation in the cognitive sphere is a balance between assimilatory and accommodatory activity, it is the fulfilment of an intention through attentional acts which are guided by, but not subordinated to, the intention. The two aspects of cognitive functioning are in reality inseparable, although they may be distinguished conceptually, and it is this fact which is responsible for the essential characteristic of intellectual advance, namely, that every cognitive achievement represents both a development from the implicit to the explicit (as the intention is fulfilled) and a development in the range of experience subtended by the categories we employ.

This theory of the process of concept formation suggests the major dimensions for the study of individual differences. There is in the first place a dimension referring to the width or narrowness of attention deployment; individuals are placed along this dimension according to their openness to new experience and their capacity to accommodate to information which, although useful to them, was not initially perceived as such. But equally important to concept formation is the drive to make the implicit explicit, to develop abstract modes of conceptualization for the ordering of experience; and individuals score along this dimension according to their ability to develop explicit analysis of stimuli. It is proposed that when a subject is functioning efficiently and extending his range of concepts, these two dimensions are complementary, since it is necessary that he should both attend to new information and articulate the meaning of it. But the possible independence of the dimensions is illustrated by those cognitive acts which do not succeed in bringing together new information and the articulation of meaning. When we are aware that the facts do not quite fit our existing concepts but are unable to say why or suggest how they might become reconciled, there exists an imbalance in favour of attention or accommodation; when, on the other hand, we adhere to our original point of view and take no heed of discrepant information, the balance is in favour of intention or assimilation. Thus, the two aspects of cognition are complementary in both an evaluative and a factual manner, because optimum development requires the co-ordination of the two and this is how concepts are in fact formed.

If this simple, two-dimensional model is correct, it is not sufficient to characterize subjects by their score along one dimension alone, for we need to know their location on both axes. Presumably, it ought to be possible to distinguish broad scanners who develop abstract, explicit concepts from broad scanners whose concepts remain at the intuitive level. It is possible that the relationship between the two dimensions varies from one level of ability to another or that they are orthogonal at all ability levels. Much more empirical work is needed if a general scheme for the description of individual differences in concept formation is to be agreed upon, however. The model outlined goes far beyond the conclusions warranted

by the available evidence, so that in the remainder of the chapter we must
be content with gleaning clues as to the accuracy and utility of the model.

Width of Attention

As Wachtel (1967) has pointed out, concepts of breadth of attention
have figured prominently in research on cognitive style, although it is by
no means clear that investigators who use this concept do so in identical
or similar ways. Gardner *et al.* (1959) developed a measure of scanning
based upon Piaget's theory of decentration (Piaget, Vinh-Bang, and Matalon, 1958; Piaget, 1969) which states that perceptual accuracy and the
overcoming of certain illusions is dependent upon the subject's capacity
to co-ordinate acts of attention, as when, for example, the older child
admits conservation through being able to "decentre" his attention from
one of the dimensions of the display. Gardner and his colleagues have
developed a number of measures of scanning ability, including recording
the movement of the subject's eyes, the time he takes to make a judgment,
number of separate centrations, etc. (Gardner and Long, 1962; Luborsky,
Blinder and Schimek, 1965). There is some evidence to suggest that these
measures are correlated although further work is needed to substantiate
this.

However, it seems clear that Gardner's dimension of "scanning control"
is distinct from other measures, such as the Stroop test (Stroop, 1953a,b)
and the Rod and Frame Test. The Stroop test consists of three separate
parts, each involving the naming of colours. In part one, the subject reads
out the names of colours printed in black ink, in part two he identifies the
colour of various stimuli, and in part three he responds by identifying the
colour of the ink in which the name of a colour is printed, the ink being
different in colour from the colour designated. The test measures, therefore, the subject's ability to ignore compelling, irrelevant cues. It would
appear that this is also an apt description of Witkin's dimension of field
dependence—independence (Witkin *et al.*, 1962), which is usually measured by tests such as the Rod and Frame Test, in which the subject,
seated in a darkened room, has to adjust an illuminated rod to the vertical
position within a frame, or the Hidden Figures Test, in which the subject
has to identify a figure hidden in a complex background. Gardner (1961)

found that field independence or articulation, as measured by these tests, is distinct from scanning. Wachtel concludes that it seems valuable to distinguish between narrow attention in the sense of limited scanning and narrow attention in the sense of reduced responsiveness to compelling irrelevant stimuli. Indeed, according to the viewpoint developed in this book, measures of field articulation appear to be more closely related to the second dimension of intentional assimilation than to the attentional accommodation dimension, for they reflect the ability to focus on the relevant stimuli rather than the ability to utilize clues which may initially be regarded as redundant.

The concept of width of attention has become particularly important in the description of the cognitive dysfunctioning typical of certain schizophrenic patients. There is evidence to suggest that such patients develop thought-disorder through admitting too much information, that is, through *overinclusion*. This is defined as the inability to preserve conceptual boundaries; ideas only distantly associated with a concept become incorporated into it, making it both more abstract and less precise. Overinclusion is, therefore, a failure to inhibit these incidental associations. Several studies, reviewed by Payne (1960), report data consistent with the hypothesis that schizophrenics overinclude in comparison with other psychiatric groups and normal subjects. Zaslow (1950), for example, used a test which consisted of 14 cards. Card 1 depicts an equilateral triangle and Card 14 a perfect circle, while in the intervening cards the shape gradually changes from a triangle to a circle. The experimenter placed the cards in order and asked the subject to indicate where the circles end and where the triangles begin. The hypothesis that schizophrenics would include more cards under each concept than a group of surgical controls was confirmed. A verbal test of overinclusion was developed by Epstein (1953). In this, 50 stimulus words are each followed by 6 response words, including the word "none". The subject is asked to underline all the response words which he considers a necessary part of the concept denoted by the stimulus word. Epstein found that a group of schizophrenics underlined significantly more words than a matched group of normal subjects with the same vocabulary level.

However, overinclusion appears to be just one aspect of schizophrenic thought disorder. For, as well as the inability to screen out irrelevant stimuli, which suggest an excessively broad scanning, schizophrenics also show the effects of excessively narrow attention. Venables (1964) has argued that, while phenomena such as overinclusion and the inability of acute patients to select among incoming stimuli represent failures of breadth of attention, other phenomena, such as decreased incidental learning, decreased size constancy and disruption of distance estimation reflect a narrowing of attention and an inability to make use of available stimuli. Watchel (1967) points out that this distinction is similar to the one he makes between narrow attention in the sense of an ability to avoid compelling irrelevant cues and narrow attention in the sense of reduced scanning. It would be mistaken, then, to characterize a patient with such symptoms as exhibiting either broad or excessively narrow attention, for his attention is both too broad and too narrow. Silverman (1964) and Broen (1966) have suggested how this apparent contradiction may be resolved by reference to the style and needs of the patient, Broen, for instance, arguing that these findings may be reconciled if one assumes that schizophrenics lack a definite hierarchy for ordering response tendencies and that chronic schizophrenics attempt to deal with this by observing fewer stimuli. This view is consistent with the work of Bannister and his colleagues who have shown that the relationship between the constructs used by thought-disordered schizophrenics to describe photographs of persons is arbitrary and shows no stability over time (Bannister, 1965), although these workers would insist that the disorder arises out of disorders of personal relationships rather than a faulty attentional mechanism, since they find that schizophrenics are as organized as other groups in sorting objects (Bannister and Salmon, 1966).

There is a vast difference, of course, between the failure to screen out irrelevant stimuli and the ability to make use of incidental cues or between an obsessive focussing upon one aspect of a situation and the ability to articulate part of the perceptual field. The difference between the adaptive and the maladaptive uses of these two kinds of attention deployment is in both cases to be found in the differing relationship between the intentional and the attentional aspects of behaviour. Broad scanning is adaptive and useful when guided by an intention which remains tacit in order for new information to be assimilated; without that tacit intention it deteriorates into mere overinclusion; similarly, the focused attention of a field independent orientation results in cognitive gain in so far as it is supported by an organization of experience which, being tacit, is the ground that is as important in the construction of the whole as is the figure, the focus of attention. And without this tacit experience it deteriorates into a rigidly narrow intention.

Concrete and Abstract Thinking

The second major dimension of individual differences that may be derived from a theory of concept formation has to do with the subject's capacity to make meanings explicit by recourse to abstract, conceptual analysis. There is widespread agreement that intellectual development in general advances from concrete understanding to abstract knowledge, Piaget (1951), most notably, demonstrating how the child is at first only able to reason effectively with concrete objects and not with abstract symbols. But this is where we have to tread most carefully since we must not suppose that there is any sharp distinction between the abstract and the concrete in terms of the properties of the objects which are used in concept formation. All objects are simultaneously concrete and abstract, for each has the character of a "thing" with physical reality and each may be classified, however intuitively or pragmatically, into some abstract scheme (the class of tables, for instance).

This idea can be illustrated with reference to the work of Heidbreder (1946, 1948). She was concerned with the order of concept formation in human development and, in order to discover whether certain types of concept are formed more easily than others, she administered a test in which the subject had to learn to associate a nonsense syllable with each of a number of different kinds of stimuli, most usually, concrete objects, such as a building or a tree, spatial forms, colours, and numerical concepts. It was found that the rank order for ease of concept formation descends from objects through forms and colours to numbers. Heidbreder concluded that it is the concrete, that which has "thing-character", which is most easily understood and that the more stimuli depart from the concrete, that is, the more abstract they become, the more intractable they are to concept formation. Pikas (1966) suggests that Heidbreder's experiments are much quoted because they appear to confirm the presupposition of "common sense" that concepts of things are acquired first and abstract concepts later. But he is very critical of these experiments and their underlying rationale. He points out that when Heidbreder talked of concrete objects she was in fact referring to drawings of concrete objects or their names, not the objects themselves, and that the "abstract" forms and numbers of the studies consisted in most cases of drawings of concrete objects which in themselves contained some abstract form or occurred in definite numbers on the stimulus cards. Pikas quotes one of Heidbreder's later studies (Heidbreder, 1949) which demonstrated how the rank order established in earlier studies could be disturbed by alteration of the salience of object, form, or colour stimuli. For example, when colour predominates and object-outline is insignificant, then sorting on the basis of colour is easier than sorting on the basis of object-outline. Heidbreder herself noted that, instead of finding a correlation between ease of concept formation and the thing-character of the stimuli, ". . . the obtained order was positively correlated with the degree of efficiency with which verbal phrases performed their *semantic function*, especially with the *explicitness* with which they referred to critical features and with the directive character of their syntactic forms" (Heidbreder, 1949, p. 306). Clearly, if ease of concept formation is a function of stimulus salience, or, as Heidbreder puts it, the extent to which the relevant stimuli can be explicitly defined, then it is no longer a question of there being an inevitable progression from the concrete to the abstract. Rather, we must inquire into the subject's ability to make explicit the dimensions with which he is confronted, for abstraction consists of making the implicit explicit.

If Heidbreder's is an incorrect account of the difference between concrete and abstract thinking, how may the distinction be defined more accurately? If the question of concreteness/abstractness is not to be settled by an appeal to the stimuli which are the elements of classification, then the difference between a concrete and an abstract response must lie in the use which the subject makes of the stimuli. To understand something concretely is to be able to make use of it in action. The concrete operational child understands conservation, transitivity, and so forth, in this sense. As Polanyi (1967) has pointed out, this form of understanding is fundamental: it is evident, for example, in the person who is learning to ride a bicycle, in the blind man using his stick to judge distances, and in the doctor attempting to interpret an X-ray photograph, for in all these instances the knowledge that is acquired is not to be described as being gained through access to explicitly formulated rules, although such may exist, but of knowing "by doing". It is this kind of understanding that Merleau-Ponty (1962) believed to be absent in the problem-solving behaviour of Schneider, the brain-damaged patient who could only cope with questions through reasoning with explicitly formulated ideas; apparently, he had lost the ability to take up the meaning of objects and events directly and concretely and was restricted to the level of abstract thinking. Of course, abstract thinking does represent an advance in many respects upon concrete thinking; as Piaget has shown, formal operational thinking is so much more flexible than concrete thinking and it results in knowledge which, because it can be explicitly formulated, can be transmitted easily from generation to generation. An abstract concept is a concrete concept made explicit; it is the articulation of a meaning that has been grasped only intuitively. But although abstraction does represent the fulfilment of concrete understanding, the two modes of thought are complementary, concrete thinking tending towards the abstract as its natural expression, abstract thinking being grounded upon the working of concrete understanding. We shall see in Chapter 10 that this theory has some significance for education since it is clear that there are important problems involved in relating different types of conceptual knowledge, some of which are more concrete, others more abstract.

The main implication of this point of view for individual differences is that we are no longer led to see concrete thinking as a totally inferior mode which is surpassed at the level of abstract ability. Although both ontogenetically and phylogenetically there is a progression from one to the other, it makes sense to characterize concrete thinking as an ability just as much as abstract thinking and, indeed, both may become liabilities under certain circumstances, for example, when abstract analysis is required and the individual remains on the level of concrete reasoning or when persistence in abstract conceptualization prevents one from taking up and utilizing the meaning of a situation. The relationship between ability and deficit is for this dimension exactly the same as for the dimension of attention deployment, where, as noted earlier, narrow attention may signify an excessive rigidity or an ability to withstand compelling irrelevant cues and broad attention deployment may signify overinclusion or the ability to make use of incidental cues. In this way our model of individual differences in concept formation allows us to relate cognitive style to ability since each cognitive style may be an ability or the lack of it.

This usage of the distinction between concrete and abstract thought, it should be noted, stands in contrast to the usage favoured by a number of clinical and social psychologists (Goldstein and Scheerer, 1941; Kasanin, 1945; Rokeach, 1951). For example, in the Goldstein–Scheerer tests of concept formation, which require the subject to sort geometrical shapes, everyday objects, and wool of different colours, concreteness is judged in entirely negative terms as (i) the inability to produce a sorting of the stimuli, (ii) an inability to use more than one classification, (iii) failure to form the objects into groups, (iv) failure to provide a precise verbal account of what has been done. It was believed that schizophrenics could be differentiated from other diagnostic groups by the presence of greater concreteness but Payne (1960), reviewing the literature on this and other tests of object-sorting, concludes that the available evidence suggests that schizophrenics as a group are "probably not abnormally concrete in the sense of being unable to form a new concept. They are, however, abnormal in the type of concepts they form. Their concepts tend to be unusual and often eccentric" (p. 243). But these tests cannot be construed as measures of concreteness/abstractness as defined above: concreteness, negatively defined, may indeed be the failure to form a concept in the sense of making explicit a concrete meaning, but, positively defined, as the capacity to take up new meanings through integrating stimuli into sequences of action, it is a fundamental process in concept formation.

These same reservations apply to the manner in which Harvey, Hunt and Schroder (1961) distinguish between various types of "conceptual system" on the basis of the concreteness–abstractness dimension. They describe the most primitive form of conceptual system as one which is directed towards structuring the environment in terms of absolutes; an individual functioning at this level thinks rigidly and by utilizing the perceptually "given". At the second level an individual is able to distinguish between such externally imposed criteria and standards set by the individual himself, whilst at the third he is able to adopt a hypothetical approach towards reality. The fourth conceptual system extends the autonomy and freedom to devise alternative ways of interpreting reality of the earlier stages. These levels of conceptualization have been assessed by a number of tests, including a Role-Taking Test which measures the subject's ability to maintain consistency when telling a story from the different points of view of a number of characters, and an Impression

Formation Test, developed by Gollin (1954, 1958), which measures the ability to make generalizations about the behaviour of a character in a film whose behaviour is inconsistent. It is apparent that these views of concreteness—abstractness are very similar to Goldstein and Scheerer's. There is also the additional notion that rigidity of conceptualization is associated with a concrete attitude.

In reply to such ideas it may be argued that possessing a concrete knowledge of something may involve great flexibility, rather than rigidity, since there is no dependence upon a set of explicitly formulated rules. Indeed, it is possible that creativity in concept formation could only occur through a concrete mode of thinking in which all is not sharply articulated. This is certainly the idea behind Freudian conceptions of regression to more primitive levels of primary process thinking in the creative process. These types of mental process are seen as allowing the person greater freedom and flexibility than the conventions of abstract thinking permit. Kris (1953) has coined the term "regression in the service of the ego" to refer to the person's capacity to utilize such processes, notably displacement, condensation, and symbolization, in a controlled and effective manner. It is arguable, therefore, that abstract thinking can also be associated with rigidity and an inability to form new ideas. What seems to be more fruitful than associating either concreteness or abstractness with rigidity is to understand the different kinds of rigidity that may occur in the progress of the concept from its beginnings in concrete experience to its fulfilment as an abstraction. Essentially this involves an examination of how creative thinking takes place.

Convergent and Divergent Thinking

The bi-polar dimension which comes closer to an integration of the two dimensions of attention deployment and concreteness/abstractness is the dimension of abilities, first proposed by Guilford (1967), which contrasts convergent and divergent ability. Convergent ability is the ability, measured by conventional tests of intelligence, to "converge" upon the correct answer to a problem, whether this demands verbal reasoning or the understanding of spatial relationships or retrieval of an item of information from memory. Tests of divergent thinking represent an attempt to measure another aspect of intellectual activity, the capacity to think of a number of possible answers to a problem for which there is not *one* correct answer. The Uses for Objects Test, for example, presents the subject with the names of a few common objects, like a brick or a button, and the subject is required to think of as many uses as possible for each object. The test is scored by taking into account the sheer number of the responses (a fluency score), the number of pre-established categories across which the subject's responses range (a flexibility score), and the number of times the subject produces a response which is unique for that sample of subjects (an originality score). Other tests, scored in a similar manner, are the Word Association Test, which requires the subject to generate as many definitions as possible to a number of stimulus words, and a Line Meanings Test in which the subject has to suggest as many meanings as possible for line-drawings. Such tests are sometimes referred to as "creativity tests" but, in the absence of convincing evidence that they do reflect an ability which is useful in genuine creativity, it is more accurate to refer to them as tests of divergent thinking.

Whilst there have been a large number of psychometric studies designed to explore the dimension of divergent thinking (see, for example, the review by Freeman, Butcher and Christie, 1971), most of these have been concerned with tests of divergent thinking alone or with the question of the relationship between divergent and convergent ability. From this work it may be tentatively concluded that divergent thinking represents an independent dimension of ability when at least two conditions are met. In the first place, the average I.Q. of the sample should be at least 120; below that level there is a significant correlation between the two. And, secondly, the divergent tests should be administered in an atmosphere which is as relaxed and "evaluation-free" as possible, for treating divergent thinking tasks as "tests" also results in a significant correlation between convergent and divergent ability. But, although this much seems reasonably clear, we know very little about the psychological processes involved in divergent production. Does the dimension of divergent thinking represent a unitary dimension of ability or are there, in fact, a number of distinct abilities involved in divergent production? Some authors (Hargreaves and Bolton, 1972) argue for the former position, others (Dacey, Madaus and Allen, 1969) for the latter. At the risk of going too far beyond the available evidence, I would like to suggest that divergent thinking is associated with the two poles of the dimensions of individual differences designated in this chapter as width of attention deployment and concreteness and that convergent thinking is associated with the opposing poles of these dimensions, namely, analytic ability and abstractness. The evidence for this contention is fragmentary but the model is proposed to stimulate research rather than to summarize an existing body of facts which have been systematically gathered.

A study which directly links divergent thinking with width of attention deployment is that of Ward (1969) who administered three divergent thinking tests, each of which required children to name as many ideas as they could for a simple problem. Ward administered two of the tests in what he called a "barren" experimental setting and, on the basis of these test results, divided the subjects into "creative" and "uncreative" subgroups. Then the third test was administered — to some subjects under the same conditions but to others in a "cue-rich" environment. Comparison of the reactions of the two subgroups to these different conditions revealed that the "uncreative" subjects were not affected by the environmental variations but the divergent thinkers produced significantly more responses in the rich than in the barren environment. Ward proposed that this was because the divergent thinker scans the environment more broadly than the convergent thinker and thus is more alert to incidental cues. It may be hypothesized that convergent thinking is associated with narrow attention, as measured by Witkin's tests of field dependence; this is the ability to focus upon the matter in hand and thus withstand compelling irrelevant cues. Witkin (1965) in fact reports that there is a relationship between the Rod-and-Frame Test and the Embedded Figures Test on the one hand and Wechsler Intelligence Scale measures of analytic ability, such as the Block Design, Picture Completion, and Object Assembly subtests (Wechsler, 1958).

Although further studies are needed to substantiate the claim that these two forms of attention deployment are characteristic of divergers and convergers, it is the relationship between convergent—divergent thinking and concreteness—abstractness which is at present purely speculative. This is because tests of concreteness—abstractness currently in use identify concreteness with rigidity or absence of concepts and fail to reflect the positive function of the concrete attitude, that of allowing the individual to respond adaptively but intuitively to novel and varying situations. But abstract conceptualization is founded upon concrete experience and unless a person is able to draw upon the concrete he will be confined to "mere abstractions". As Elton Mayo (1945) puts it (quoted by Rogers (1965) in *Client-Centered Therapy*, p. 16):

"Speaking historically, I think it can be asserted that a science has generally come into being as a product of well-developed technical skill in a given area of activity. Someone, some skilled worker, has in a reflective moment attempted to make explicit the assumptions that are implicit in the skill itself. This makes the beginning of logico-experimental method. The assumptions once made explicit can be logically developed; the development leads to experimental changes of practice and so to the beginning of a science. The point to be remarked is that scientific abstractions are not drawn from thin air or uncontrolled reflection; they are from the beginning rooted deeply in a pre-existent skill" (p. 17).

Concrete knowledge is knowledge in action; it consists of *knowing how to do something* so that, although one may not be able to formulate the principles upon which the actions are based, changing circumstances can be tackled skilfully and creatively. If broad attention deployment and analytic ability represent two styles for accommodating to the demands of the environment, concreteness and abstractness are the two major ways in which the person imposes a meaning upon that environment; in the former events are assimilated into an action system and in the latter into a system of abstract categories. Psychologists have been able to construct tests of abstract reasoning without a great deal of difficulty but have not yet addressed themselves to measuring that openness to experience which is at the heart of concrete understanding.

It is suggested that the quality of openness to concrete experience is one of the major psychological processes measured by the majority of traditional tests of divergent thinking. The divergent thinker extracts meaning from the stimuli presented to him, not by subsuming aspects of them into well-defined categories, but by responding to some particular, concrete characteristic, as, for example, when a child says that one of the uses for a button is for it to serve as a hatch on a toy submarine, or is able to see a certain meaning in a line drawing or a nonsense word. It is this capacity of elaborating concrete meanings through incorporating aspects of experience into a potential activity or purpose that is the essence of divergent thinking and it is in this crucial respect that such thinking stands opposed to convergent thinking which organizes stimuli into classes and relations through abstract rules.

In summary, two dimensions of individual differences in concept formation are proposed corresponding to the attentional and intentional aspects of experience. These are termed attention deployment and concreteness—abstractness. It is argued that the two poles of each dimension may be characterized both positively and negatively. Thus broad attention deployment may signify a responsiveness to available cues or mere overinclusion and narrow attention deployment may be the capacity to withstand compelling, irrelevant stimuli or mere rigidity of purpose. Similarly, a concrete attitude may imply the capacity to take up particular meanings through incorporating stimuli into schemes of action or a meaningless preoccupation with concrete characteristics, while abstractness may represent the success of relating elements into higher order series or the failure to come to grips with the properties of the task in hand. The cognitive style of convergent thinking is viewed as embodying narrow attention deployment together with an abstract attitude, whilst divergent thinking involves broad attention deployment and concreteness. Each of these abilities may be relevant at some stage in concept formation and we may, therefore, look forward to the day when we can describe individual differences in concept formation according to a scheme which corresponds to what is known about the process of concept formation.

PART III

IMPLICATIONS

CHAPTER 10

Concept Formation and
Educational Practice

This account of concept formation has so far been concerned with describing the course of conceptual development and with explanations of the ways in which concepts are learned. The present chapter treads more dangerous ground for it is concerned not only with matters of fact but with questions of value, that is, with establishing what *ought to be* in the context of what *is*. Thus in the present chapter our central preoccupation is the educationalist's question: how should teaching be adjusted to the conceptual level of the child and the ways in which he most effectively learns concepts? It is obvious that this question is not one that can be answered by a direct appeal to the facts of development and learning because the teacher's intention is not to conform to any scientific laws that may be established about these matters; rather, it is to use his knowledge of these laws in order to *improve* those under his care. As Bruner (1966) has argued, theories of learning and of development are descriptive rather than prescriptive; they tell us that, for example, most children of nine or ten possess an understanding of conservation of weight. A theory of instruction, on the other hand, would be concerned with establishing the best means of leading the child towards this understanding — with improving rather than describing learning. Bruner contends, then, that prescriptive theories of instruction must be congruent with descriptive theories of psychological development.

Whilst I believe no one would wish to dispute this, it may well be that this formulation underestimates the difficulties of joining the two together. The assertion that a theory of instruction might be concerned with devising the best means of attaining concepts, such as conservation, may be construed as implying that a theory of instruction is solely to do with

131

means to established ends: it is taken for granted in our example that it is desirable that the child acquires as efficiently as possible a knowledge of conservation. Now, if we could take for granted what has to be learned, but only if we could, a theory of instruction would deal exclusively with means. But once it is admitted that various values underlie the selection of educational knowledge and that it is by no means clear which values should prevail, then a theory of instruction cannot seek security by adopting the status of a technology but must become involved in wider questions about the nature of the values that determine in large part *what* is taught. And in the absence of definitive answers to these questions any psychology of instruction must be a very provisional affair.

However, it remains true that the psychology of concept formation could be of service to the teacher in the attainment of his immediate goals. Bruner says that a theory of instruction has four major features. In the first place, it should specify the experiences which implant in the individual a predisposition towards learning. Secondly, it must specify the ways in which knowledge is to be structured so that it can be grasped by the learner; such structuring must of course take into account the learner's abilities. Third, a theory of instruction should specify the most effective sequences in which to present the materials to be learned. Fourth, it should specify the nature and sequence of the rewards and punishments in the process of learning and teaching. The first and fourth of these features have to do with motivation and learning directly, while the second and third relate to problems of curriculum organization. In line with the preoccupation of this account of concept formation, it may be suggested that there are two further features of equal importance. There is, in the first place, the large question of individual differences and how teaching methods can be adjusted to the different cognitive styles of individuals. And, finally, there is the question of education for creativity: Bruner's four features appear to place too much emphasis upon the learner's acquisition of already established knowledge and not enough upon the development of the disposition and ability to discover for oneself. Jones (1968) has criticized Bruner on this count, asserting that he has focussed upon concept attainment to the neglect of concept formation.

It may be helpful if we summarize our conclusions with respect to these four areas of concept formation: organization of the material to be learned, the motivation for concept learning, creativity in formation, and individual differences.

(1) *Organization of material.* One of the most fundamental aspects of Piaget's theory of intellectual development is the idea that there are two distinguishable types of knowledge, logico-mathematical and physical knowledge. The latter refers to the understanding of the properties inherent in the environment, as when, for example, one learns something about the composition of a particular specimen of rock, whilst the former refers to the understanding of the actions and operations by which objects or their symbols are related, as, for example, when the child learns that subtraction reverses addition. In physical knowledge what is learned is something about the nature of the object itself, while in logico-mathematical knowledge what is learned is something about the interrelations between our actions or operations (which are internalized systems of actions). But, although these two types of experience are capable of being distinguished conceptually, in the course of intellectual development they are inseparable, since it is by adapting to the properties of his environment that the child develops operational skills and, reciprocally, it is through the development of these skills that the child knows more about his environment. This close relationship between physical experience or figurative knowledge and operational knowledge is of the greatest significance for educational practice since it implies that there are a number of stages through which the learning of any subject-matter proceeds. The problem of teaching is then, in part at least, that of identifying these stages so that the learner can be brought successfully from one to the next. As we shall see in a moment, this problem has been most thoroughly documented with respect to mathematics learning but it manifests itself with any subject-matter which is taught over a number of developmental levels. Thus, Goldman (1964) has shown that there are a number of stages in the development of religious concepts, and Jahoda (1963) that the young child's understanding of geographical locations is typically limited, since he does not possess yet an adequate understanding of class-inclusion and cannot, therefore, work out the relationships between cities and countries. Clearly, the teacher should be aware of such limitations and structure his lessons to overcome them. The material he presents should be both comprehensible and stimulate the child to advance his thinking. It is here that the sequence in which the material is presented is crucial. One suspects that in the learning of mathematics failure is often due to some important step in the sequence not being fully mastered by the student.

(2) *Motivation for concept learning.* The presentation of the material in its proper sequence is important also if the learner is to develop and retain an interest in the subject. The purpose of devising and teaching according to a sequence of acquisitions is to enable the learner to respond to new information by an act of organization. The learner is able to organize the material because the material relates to his existing knowledge. The material may be such that it leads to an extension of the learner's cognitive structures, as in concept formation, or the material may provide the learner with an opportunity for consolidating an already-established concept, as in concept attainment. In either case it is, in Hunt's (1961) terms, the "match" between the learner's repertoire of skills and the nature of the material which is decisive for the development of an intrinsic motivation to attain competence in the subject: ideally the congruence between his expectations and the environmental event confirms his competence while incongruity extends it. Ideally so, of course, and not always actually, since the congruence may slip into mere rote learning and the incongruence may be just too much for the learner to handle. Put in this form, it is not a matter of opposing one of these kinds of learning to the other in the way that "discovery learning" has been contrasted to rote learning, for expansion and consolidation of learning are two aspects of the same process.

(3) *Creativity in concept formation.* But the process by which new concepts are formed is very poorly understood, for the idea of an optimal match between experience and environment or Piaget's notion of equilibration point more to the conditions which promote conceptual growth than to the psychological mechanisms involved in that growth. In Chapter 3 we resorted to an analysis of the experience of concept formation, that is, to phenomenology, in order to clarify this problem. There, it was concluded that the capacity to attend to and utilize incidental cues is an important feature of creative thinking and the more alert the person is to cues existing on the "fringe" of consciousness, the more chance he has of forming new concepts. Stout used the term, apperception, to refer to the process, referred to later by Piaget as equilibration, by which the subject adjusts to conditions which are partly familiar and partly unfamiliar (Stout, 1902; Piaget, 1951). We saw that others, notably Merleau-Ponty (1962) and Polanyi (1959), took up this line of thought, distinguishing between tacit and explicit knowledge, and argued that explicit knowledge rests upon a framework of tacit knowledge. What is crucial in all these accounts

is the idea that learning depends upon the person successfully relating his *present* intentions and actions to his past experience. It is here, surely, that the so-called "new methods" in education, which emphasize learning by discovery and capitalizing upon the child's own motivation, make their most valid contribution, for the act of discovery is the act by which the learner relates himself, that is, his own interests and knowledge, to a new experience. It is, therefore, untrue to state, as Gardner (1969) does, that such methods have no clearly argued rationale. There are very good, psychological, reasons to support the practice of arranging conditions of learning so that subjects begin from the vantage-point of their own experience in order that they can make sense of new knowledge.

The second major criticism that can be levelled against teaching which does not take into account the motives and previous experience of the learner but attempts to drill him in facts which are presented as already established, is that it inhibits the development of wide attention deployment. Because the learner's attention is focussed solely upon the topic selected by the teacher, or, more specifically, because the teacher demands a response from the child which indicates that he has learned what he was meant to learn, there will be minimal use of incidental cues in furthering the child's understanding of the topic. As Stenild (1972) asserted, in the first stage of concept learning one must not demand specific reactions from the subject in the shape of an immediate categorizing activity, since it is through global scanning that the learner relates past to present experience in an ordered whole. The failure of rote learning lies in its suppression of tacit knowing.

(4) *Individual differences.* But the teacher does not deal in reality with "the learner" but with individual learners and must, therefore, be sensitive to the ways in which individuals differ. Although many dimensions of individual differences have been proposed, it was suggested in Chapter 9 that no great injustice would be done to our existing knowledge if we were to restrict ourselves to two broad dimensions, attention deployment and concreteness—abstractness. It was argued that the relationship between cognitive style (obtained by plotting an individual on these axes) and cognitive ability is jointly determined by the nature of the style and the requirements of the task. For example, broad attention deployment could signify an alertness to available cues or overinclusion, whilst narrow attention deployment could refer to the ability to withstand compelling,

irrelevant cues or rigidity of purpose; similarly, that a concrete attitude could signify the employment of tacit knowing or a too-restricting pre-occupation with concrete details, while abstractness could be the ability to form explicit categories or a failure to accommodate to the concrete characteristics of the task. The relevance of work on cognitive styles for education lies not only in it alerting the teacher to individual differences in the ways in which problems are tackled but also in the fact that it has led several authors (Getzels and Jackson, 1962; Hudson, 1968) to argue that traditional methods of teaching are far too oriented to certain types of personality. In particular, it is argued that the cognitive style of the con-vergent thinker, which in our terms may be characterized as a combina-tion of abstractness and focussed attention, appears to be especially fa-voured by traditional education, and not enough has been done to favour those skills fostered by divergent thinking with its components of broad attention deployment and concreteness. If this is the case, new methods in education which avoid the limitations of traditional methods should be more consistent with the attributes of the divergent thinker.

These, then, are the generalizations suggested by theory and research into concept formation. There is, of course, a large leap from such abstrac-tions as these to the concrete, teaching situation and it will surely always be true that the psychologist's knowledge is abstract, while the teacher has the more difficult task of integrating practice in the concrete situation with his knowledge of general rules. Moreover, there are, no doubt, problems of instruction specific to each academic discipline which will make it impos-sible to state any detailed sequence of teaching that is true for all subjects. But a great many changes involving both curriculum and teaching method have occurred in the last few years and some research into the effects of different practices on success in specific disciplines has been carried out. In the remainder of this chapter, therefore, we shall examine these changes and the research work carried out to assess them. We shall be concerned particularly with mathematics learning, since it is with this subject that the most explicit links between psychological theory and educational practice have been drawn, but we shall also look at concept learning in social studies, partly because the content of this discipline is quite different and offers an alternative case-study in the relationship between psychology and education, and partly because it provides an excellent example of how the "new methods" involve both new methods and new content.

Forming Mathematical Concepts

There is widespread agreement among psychologists who have investigated mathematical concept formation about the inadequacies of traditional stimulus-response learning theory and the need for a theory of structured learning. Biggs (1967) asserts the necessity of constructing a theory which will account for the process by which the learner acquires meaning or structure, rather than a response or action, and draws upon Piagetian theory for this purpose. Skemp (1963) distinguishes between primary and secondary concepts: a primary concept is derived directly from sensory experience, whereas a secondary concept is derived from other concepts; for instance, the concept of "dog" is primary because the child can only acquire it by having direct acquaintance with a number of examples, but the concept of "animal" is secondary in the sense that it is derived from the child's prior knowledge of various kinds of animals, such as dogs, cats, etc. For Skemp, some mathematical concepts, such as "three", are primary, since they are formed through inspection of collections of three objects, while others are secondary for they consist of generalizations about the properties of individual numbers. Thus, $8 \times 7 = 56$ is understandable on the primary conceptual level, whilst $8(x+y) = 8x + 8y$ is a secondary concept. Skemp believes that many of the difficulties experienced in mathematics learning stem from the transition from primary to secondary modes of representation and understanding and he proposes a schematic theory of learning to account for the way in which successful instruction should progress from structured primary to structured secondary knowledge. Although the distinction between primary and secondary concepts is derived from the empiricist philosophy of Locke, rather than the operationalist theory of Piaget, the main features of Skemp's theory of schematic learning are essentially Piagetian. He talks, for instance, of assimilation of events to the schema and its accommodation to new facts.

Dienes (1963) argues for the existence of a number of stages in mathematical concept formation. In the first stage, the person's behaviour is playful and haphazard, at the second it becomes more regular and purposeful, but it is confined to practice in handling situations in which the rule-structure of the subject-matter is relevant and results in a more or less unconscious stamping-in of the rule; at the third stage, analytic thinking about the rule becomes possible: it exists now as an object of thought.

F

When a number of new objects of thought have been constructed, Dienes maintains that the cycle of thought can begin again, since we need to manipulate them freely in order to find out just what we can do with them. Dienes calls this process a "Piaget cycle" since the three stages correspond to the Piagetian notions of intuitive play, concrete understanding and abstract reasoning. He has attempted to embody these stages in the procedures he has devised to advance mathematics learning. For each mathematical concept there is a progression from what he calls an experience game with little or no structure, through a structured game, which is aimed at providing the child with insight into the nature of the concept. One of the most important parts of Dienes' apparatus is the Multibase Arithmetic Blocks, which consists of a series of blocks which are structured in geometrical progression to the third power in constant multiples of 3, 4, 5, 6, and 10. The basic purpose of the blocks is to enable the child to understand the concept of place value in relation to the operations of addition, subtraction, multiplication and division. Bases other than ten are used because of the view that in order to have a proper understanding of the concept of place value it is necessary for the child to experience a number of exemplars, other than merely illustrating one example of it – the decimal system. It is in this respect that the Dienes apparatus differs most significantly from other structural methods, notably the Stern blocks and Cuisenaire rods which provide only one example of the concept to be learned; in the latter, for example, the child associates numbers with colours (adding brown to red to produce orange, say) and is intended to internalize his actions with the rods so that he develops logical operations.

At the present time, then, there are a number of different methods in use in the classroom for teaching mathematical concepts. There are the traditional methods with their emphasis upon repetition, the early use of symbolism, computational efficiency and extrinsic motivation. In contrast to these methods, in discovery learning the aim is to motivate the child to develop understanding on the basis of his own experience, and the emphasis is upon wide experience, the gradual introduction of numerical symbols only after concrete experience with numerical relationships, problem solving rather than computation, and intrinsic motivation. And, finally, there are specific methods, such as the Dienes blocks and Cuisenaire rods, for use in the development of certain basic concepts. In Britain, the Nuffield Mathematics Project, following closely the ideas of Piaget, has developed techniques of instruction and methods of assessment for a wide range of concepts, for example, transitivity, conservation. The whole impetus of the "new mathematics" is, therefore, to develop fundamental operations to begin with so that the child can grasp the interconnectedness and the logical progression of the subject.

However, judged in the light of research findings, which of these methods is the most successful in promoting an understanding of mathematical concepts is still an open question. Biggs (1967) reports a study of over 5,000 children in their third year at junior school. These children were given a battery of tests which included an intelligence test as well as tests of mechanical arithmetic and arithmetical problems involving reasoning and problem solving. The heads of the schools supplied details of the way in which each child had been taught and Biggs classified these methods into three main groups: traditional, structural, and motivational. The structural group was subdivided into two further groups which Biggs called uni-model (Stern and Cuisenaire), in which, it will be recalled, the child learns the concept from experience of one kind of example of it, and multi-model (Dienes), in which the concept is learned through a variety of exemplars. He characterized motivational methods as such because the main emphasis in teaching is the interest and everyday relevance of problems rather than their logical structure. Biggs hypothesized that the traditional methods of teaching should be more successful with respect to tests of mechanical arithmetic, whereas structural and possibly motivational methods would surpass the traditional when conceptual understanding, rather than rote learning, was demanded. In fact, he found very little difference in the performance of children, whether mechanical or conceptual, who had been trained by traditional and uni-model, structural methods, although there was a tendency for the more intelligent children to benefit from uni-model methods, as against the less intelligent, whilst the duller and average children made relatively greater progress with the Dienes multi-model methods. In general, when intelligence was held constant, the multi-model approach produced significantly better results on both the mechanical and conceptual test items and Biggs suggests that this indicates that these children were responding to the mechanical items with insight, since they had virtually no experience of rote learning. Exclusive use of motivational methods was found to produce poor attainment at all intelligence levels, but Biggs noted the possibility that such methods may induce greater enthusiasm and originality, especially in brighter children. The available evidence relating to this possibility is, however, equivocal. Haddon and Lytton (1968) have demonstrated that the informal atmosphere generated by discovery methods does produce significant gains on tests of divergent thinking, and this finding is consistent with work in this area showing the benefits of a relaxed atmosphere for divergent thinking (Wallach and Kogan, 1965). But it does not follow that if a child is successful on such tests he will be successful on tests which require *both* originality *and* finding an answer that is correct. Richards and Bolton (1971), therefore, devised a number of mathematical tests which assessed this ability and administered them along with tests of mechanical arithmetic, intelligence, and divergent thinking in order to explore the relationships between these abilities. On the basis of their results they concluded that divergent thinking contributes only minimally to performance on tests of mathematics, including those demanding originality. However, other studies (Hasan and Butcher, 1966) have reported significant correlations between tests of arithmetic and divergent thinking, so that, as a recent review of the literature (Bennett, 1973) makes clear, further work is needed to clarify the role of divergent thinking and its relationship to academic attainment.

Other studies have been concerned with demonstrating how the implementation of specific training programmes can accelerate learning and understanding. Bruner and Kenney (1965) gave intensive training to four 8-year-old children who had I.Q.s in the region of 120 to 130. The children were taught quadratic equations through techniques which were very similar to those used by Dienes, and which placed the emphasis upon the child working from the concrete embodiment of mathematical relations in apparatus such as balance beams and squares of wood to an understanding of how these relations can be represented symbolically. Bruner and Kenney noted that the children always began, when confronted with a problem, by constructing an embodiment of some concept, creating what they called "a concrete form of operational definition". The result of this construction was thus an image and some operations which "stood for" the concept. Subsequently, the problem was to provide means of representation that were independent of particular manipulations and images, that is, symbolic representation. However, this is not to say that at this stage imagery becomes completely redundant, since it is probable, they argue, that the able mathematician continues to rely upon some imagery to provide him with a rough and ready guide which can be supplemented when needs be by more rigorous procedures. Whilst Bruner and Kenney have shown how intensive, individual training can accelerate the learning of abstract concepts in young children, Skemp (1971) reports a study which demonstrated the advantages of schematic as opposed to rote learning both for understanding and retention with a group of Grammar School boys. He devised for the purpose of the experiment an artificial schema which consisted of 16 basic signs which could be combined, in the manner of Red Indian sign language, to convey a variety of meanings. On the first day of the experiment the subjects learnt the meanings of these signs and on subsequent days they learnt the meanings of various combinations of the signs. Thus, three basic signs are:

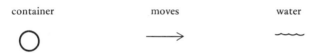

and these may be combined to give, for example:

The final task for the subjects was to learn two pages of symbols, the symbols being arranged in groups of 8 to 10. On one page, each group of symbols was given a meaning related to the meanings of smaller groups with which the subject was familiar, but the other page contained groups which were meaningful to a comparison sample of subjects but not to these subjects. This was because the comparison group had learned the same symbols but with different meanings, so that each group of subjects had an appropriate schema for one page and an inappropriate schema for the other. Skemp found very significant differences between schematic and rote learning both for initial and long-term recall. Although both Skemp's and Bruner and Kenney's studies involved above-average ability subjects, it is very probable that their results are generalizable to all ability ranges.

In summary, whilst specific training programmes, such as those of Skemp and Bruner and Kenney, which are based upon psychological principles, do show a measure of success, the validation of new methods as used in the normal classroom can only be regarded as incomplete. Biggs's study provides some support for the use of methods which provide a variety of exemplars of the same concept, for example, the approach of Dienes, but the value of learning through discovery in terms of greater comprehension and intrinsic motivation has not been firmly established. It does appear likely, however, that discovery learning will be found to be just one means for the acquisition of knowledge, rather than the only means, and the problem will be one of discovering what sort of knowledge is best taught through discovery and what sort through a reliance upon deduction or supplied information.

Forming Concepts in Social Science

One of the major motives for change in the teaching of mathematics and science has undoubtedly been the view that traditional methods led quite often to a failure on the part of the learner to understand the relevant concepts. Similarly, in the field of social studies, that is, in all those subjects which have to do with the nature of man and his development, there has been a movement away from the rote learning of facts towards teaching which stresses the interrelationships between facts. Writing about the teaching of such subjects in the United States, Martorella (1971) states that curricula have been organized according to the chronological sequence of events or the topical themes within a given period. He argues that this practice conflicts with the generalization that may be gleaned from models of concept learning, namely, that the structure and character of facts are more important in organizing instruction than their place in a temporal sequence. "Whether facts interrelate as exemplars and are devoid of non-exemplars takes precedence over their chronological sequence or topical relationship" (p. 88). He quotes a number of examples of the application of principles derived from psychological models to topics within social studies.

A much more ambitious attempt, since it involves the development of a new course, is reported by Bruner (1966). The course, called "Man: a course of study", aims to define man in an evolutionary context. According to Bruner, three questions recur throughout the course: what is human about human beings? How did they get that way? How can they be made more so? The plan is to present children with exercises and materials by which they can learn about both similarities and dissimilarities between man and other animals. In pursuit of this goal, five major themes are explored, each of which represents the distinctiveness of man and his capacity for further progress. These themes are tool-making, language, social organization, the management of man's prolonged childhood, and man's urge to explain the world. These are interconnected themes (for example, the invention of tools has implications for the division of labour) and the aim of the teacher is to instil in the child the most general and basic understanding of them. Thus, the section on social organization has the objective of making children aware of the existence of social structures and how these are subject to change. One means of inducing this awareness is to have the children compare their own customs with those of another society, such as Eskimos or Bushmen. As Bruner puts it: ". . . we hope to achieve for our pupils a sense of continuity by first presenting them with what seems like contrast and letting them live with it long enough to sense wherein what before seemed bizarrely different is, in fact, closely akin to things they understand from their own lives" (pp. 93–4). Indeed, many of the customs of the Netsilik Eskimos that the children witness on film are far removed from Western society: hunting for seals with spears, leaving the old to die when they are no longer capable of looking after themselves, are quite novel experiences for a child reared in Western society. Bruner argues that the child works through such experiences to a realization of the order and integrity of different societies and the continuities between them. Jones (1968), on the other hand, believes that such teaching runs the considerable risk of interfering with children's emotions without a very clear idea of the damage that could be done. He raises the vital point that, whereas in teaching mathematics or science, the nature of the subject permits the use of learning through discovery and active involvement without the risk of serious consequences for personality functioning, teaching about the nature of man in this way, if it is successful, necessarily involves the whole personality.

Classification and Framing

We see that in two distinct fields of knowledge, mathematics and social studies, there are two major changes in the teaching of concepts. The one refers directly to the contents of teaching. In both fields there is an increasing emphasis placed upon concepts that are sufficiently general to afford a basis for integrating facts and principles which were previously kept separate or only acquired at more advanced levels: the early introduction of notions of sets in mathematics is a good example of this; the course reported by Bruner yet another, since historical, geographical and cultural phenomena are viewed as a whole. The second change refers to the manner in which information is transmitted. Bruner sums up the general feeling here when he says that it is of little use to give information that is not asked for. He means, of course, that the learner must recognize the possible relevance and usefulness of any information if it is to mean anything to him. Successful learning is, therefore, the result of questioning and discovery. Bernstein (1971) refers to these two changes in the transmission of educational knowledge as changes in classification and framing. Classification denotes the degree to which subjects and subject-matter are distinguished from one another: strong classification exists when boundaries between disciplines are adhered to, weak classification when attempts are made to integrate teaching across disciplines. Psychologically, the distinction may be stated as one between independent and integrated conceptual systems. The concept of framing refers to the strength of the boundary between what may and may not be transmitted: strong framing indicates a sharp boundary between the two, weak framing indicates a blurred boundary, that is, teacher and taught participate in the control of what is learned. From the point of view of the psychology of learning, the difference between strong and weak framing is the difference between acquiring concepts which are presented as firmly established and unchallengable and participating in a process by which one forms one's own concepts to make sense of reality. Theoretically, classification and framing can vary independently of one another (there can be, for example, weak classification but strong framing) but proponents of new methods in teaching would argue for the advantages of weak classification and weak framing.

CHAPTER 11

Theoretical Implications

The first section of the book was an attempt to indicate the kinds of phenomena that need to be accounted for by an adequate psychological theory of concept formation. We began by noting the opposition between two accounts of concept formation, the inductive and the deductive, and argued in Chapter 2 that the relationship between the terms of our analysis should not be one of opposition but of complementarity: attention and intention, the general and the particular, and logico-mathematical and physical experience are complementary aspects of experience, we concluded, because concept formation, like all development, progresses through the person developing his models of reality (whether these are called constructs, concepts or cognitive structures) at the same time that he adapts to the demands of that reality. It was maintained that a concept is formed through the subject's activity of identifying stimuli as instances of a type or rule. Such a view is evident in certain philosophical critiques of the traditional theory of abstraction. The important lesson to be learnt from these critiques and especially from phenomenological accounts is that concept formation is not fundamentally a process by which resemblances are subsumed under explicit categories, as the traditional theory held, but a process in which stimuli are transformed into instances by the application of a rule, whether tacit or explicit. The importance of tacit knowledge was emphasized in Chapter 3 which made special reference to Merleau-Ponty's views on cognition, whilst in Chapter 4, I suggested a typology of concepts and examined the possibility that conceptual systems may divide into qualitatively different modes of thought.

One of the intentions which animated the theoretical exposition of Part I was the desire to show — without reference to what psychologists have actually done — the extent of the field of study subsumed by the topic

145

label, Concept Formation, thereby avoiding the textbook writer's error of identifying what psychologists should study with what they actually do study. Perhaps, then, it is inevitable that in reviewing empirical work on concept formation in Part II one should be aware of a disparity between the two. For example, having subjects learn that the correct response is "all red triangles with blue borders" may have been methodologically useful in externalizing the processes involved in concept formation, but the ease with which this sort of experiment can be carried out may well have led us to take too narrow a view of human conceptual behaviour. In this respect there are a number of outstanding questions. For example, the area suffers from a lack of integration of approaches, with work in the developmental tradition being theoretically isolated from work on concept formation in adults; there has been no attempt to understand the possibly different conceptual structures involved, say, in scientific, aesthetic and evaluative-philosophical modes of thought; or again, to what extent can we generalize from our observations of subjects' strategies in experimental tasks to their strategies in the world outside the laboratory? If we are to progress to a more comprehensive psychology of concept formation, issues such as these will have to be faced.

However, the purpose of this book has not been merely to sound a warning-note to the experimental psychology of concept formation. The more fundamental purpose has been to suggest that there can and must be some form of agreement between on the one hand conceptual and phenomenological analysis of conceptual behaviour, and on the other hand the results of developmental and experimental investigations. And there are some encouraging pointers in this direction. Thus the study of pre-conceptual development has traced the emergence of the sense of the identity of objects, an achievement stressed in phenomenological analysis as fundamental in cognition. There has also been a growing awareness of the variety of rules which concepts can exemplify (see, for example, Bourne, 1970) and this parallels the criticism made against the traditional theory of abstraction that it placed too much reliance upon the principle of class inclusion and ignored the many other logical rules which organize our concepts. Again, the pioneering work of Bruner, Goodnow and Austin (1956) may be viewed as a reformulation at a more operational level of the ideas of Cassirer (1923) and others on the predictive nature of the concept, for in both formulations the concept learner's task is to determine the attributes that serve to predict whether a stimulus is an instance of a type. The distinction between "new" and "old" methods of instruction in Chapter 10 and the distinction between cognitive and associationist modes of learning in Chapter 7 were perhaps too sharply drawn in relation to a growing recognition that the long-term learning process occurring within an educational setting requires the integration of activity methods, in which children are allowed to explore for themselves without suffering evaluation from "outside", with more formal instruction which builds upon the child's own discoveries in order to expand his knowledge. It remains the task of further research to suggest how this integration might best take place. To succeed in this kind of research we shall need to combine the rigour of empirical methodology with a sensitivity to the concept formation that can occur within the environment of the classroom, determining for instance the optimum ways in which the teacher can follow up the results of a child's unstructured activity.

References

Arnheim, R. (1970), *Visual Thinking*, London: Faber.

Bandura, A. and Walters, R. H. (1965), *Social Learning and Personality Development*, New York: Holt, Rinehart & Winston.

Bannister, D. (1965), The genesis of schizophrenic thought disorder: re-test of the serial invalidation hypothesis, *Brit. J. Psychiat.*, **111**, 377.

Bannister, D. and Salmon, P. (1966), Schizophrenic thought disorder: specific or diffuse? *Brit. J. Med. Psychol.*, **39**, 215–19.

Bartlett, F. C. (1932), *Remembering*, Cambridge: Cambridge Univ. Press.

Bennett, S. N. (1973), Divergent thinking abilities: a validation study. *Brit. J. Educ. Psychol.*, **43**, 1–7.

Berger, P. L. (1970), The Problem of Multiple Realities: Alfred Schutz and Robert Musil, in M. Natanson (ed.), *Phenomenology and Social Reality*, The Hague: M. Nijhoff.

Berlyne, D. E. (1960), *Conflict, Arousal, and Curiosity*, New York: McGraw-Hill.

Berstein, B. (1971), On the classification and framing of educational knowledge, in M. F. D. Young (ed.), *Knowledge and Control*, London: Collier-Macmillan.

Beth, E. W. and Piaget, J. (1966), *Mathematical Epistemology and Psychology*, The Netherlands: Reidel.

Biggs, J. B. (1967), *Mathematics and the Conditions of Learning*, Slough: NFER.

Bolton, N. (1972), *The Psychology of Thinking*, London: Methuen.

Bourne, L. E. (1965), *Human Conceptual Behaviour*, Boston: Allyn & Bacon.

Bourne, L. E. (1970), Knowing and using concepts, *Psychol. Rev.*, **77**, 546–56.

Bourne, L. E. and Dominowski, R. L. (1972), Thinking, *Annual Review of Psychology*, **23**, Palo Alto: Annual Reviews Inc., pp. 105–30.

Bourne, L. E. and Guy, D. E. (1968), Learning conceptual rules: 1 Some interrule transfer effects, *J. Exp. Psychol.*, **76**, 423–9.

Bourne, L. E., Ekstrand, B. R. and Dominowski, R. L. (1971), *The Psychology of Thinking*, Englewood Cliffs, New Jersey: Prentice-Hall.

Bower, G. and Trabasso, T. R. (1964), Concept identification. In Atkinson, R. C. (Ed). *Studies in Mathematical Psychology*. Stanford: Stanford University Press, pp. 32–95.

Bower, T. G. R. (1971), The object in the world of the infant, *Sci. Amer.*, **225**, 4, 30–8.

Brierley, D. W. (1966), Children's use of personality constructs, *Bull. Brit. Psychol. Soc.*, **19**, no. 65, 72.

Broen, W. E. (1966), Response disorganisation and breadth of observation in schizophrenia, *Psychol. Rev.*, **73**, 579–85.

Brown, R. (1970), *Psycholinguistics*, New York: Free Press.

Bruner, J. S. (1959), Inhelder's and Piaget's "The Growth of Logical Thinking", A Psychologists Viewpoint, *Brit. J. Psychol.*, **50**, 363–7.

Bruner, J. S. (1966), *Toward a Theory of Instruction*, London: Oxford Univ. Press.

Bruner, J. S. and Kenney, H. J. (1965), Representation and mathematics learning in mathematics learning, *Monogr. Soc. Res. Child. Devel.*, **30**, 50–9.

Bruner, J. S., Goodnow, J. L. and Austin, G. A. (1956), *A Study of Thinking*, New York: Wiley.

Bruner, J. S., Olver, R. R. and Greenfield, P. M. (1966), *Studies in Cognitive Growth*, New York: Wiley.

Bryant, P. E. (1971), Cognitive development, in A. Summerfield (ed.), Cognitive Psychology, *Brit. Medical Bull.*, **27**, No. 3.

Cassirer, E. (1923), *Substance and Function and Einstein's Theory of Relativity*, Open Court: Chicago.

Cassirer, E. (1953), *The Philosophy of Symbolic Forms, Vol. 3, Phenomenology of Knowledge*, New Haven: Yale Univ. Press.

Cohen, G. M. (1967), Conservation of quantity in children: the effect of vocabulary and participation, *Quart. J. Exp. Psychol.*, **19**, 150–4.

Cohen, J. (1967), *Psychological Time in Health and Disease*, Springfield, Illinois: Thomas.

Collingwood, R. G. (1924), *Speculum Mentis*, Oxford: Clarendon Press.

Collingwood, R. G. (1933), *An Essay on Psychological Method*, Oxford: Clarendon Press.

Collingwood, R. G. (1940), *Metaphysics*, Oxford: Clarendon Press.

Dacey, J., Madaus, G. and Allen, A. (1969), The relationship of creativity and intelligence in Irish adolescents, *Brit. J. Ed. Psychol.*, **39**, 261–6.

Dale, R. S. (1972), *Language Development: Structure and Function*, Illinois: The Dryden Press.

Dewey, J. (1896), The reflex arc concept in psychology, *Psychol. Rev.*, **3**, 357–70.

Dewey, J. (1930), *The Quest for Certainty*, London: Allen & Unwin.

Dienes, Z. P. (1963), *An Experimental Study of Mathematics Learning*, London: Hutchinson.

Douvan, E. and Adelson, J. (1966), *The Adolescent Experience*, New York: Wiley.

Epstein, S. (1953), Overinclusive thinking in a schizophrenic and a control group. *J. Cons. Psychol.*, **17**, 384–88.

Erikson, E. H. (1950), *Childhood and Society*, New York: W. W. Norton & Co.

Freeman, J., Butcher, H. J. and Christie, T. (1971), *Creativity: A Selective Review of Research* (2nd ed.), London: S.R.H.E.

Frege, G. (1884), *Die Grundlagen der Arithmetik*, Breslau: W. Koebner.

Frege, G. (1918), Der Gedanke, in *Beiträge zur Philosophie des deutschen Idealismus*, I (translated by A. and M. Quinton, *Mind.*, **65** (1956)).

Friebergs, V. and Tulving, E. (1961), The effect of practice on utilization of information from positive and negative instances in concept identification, *Can. J. Psychol.*, **15**, 101–6.

Freud, S. (1915), *The Unconscious*, in Vol. 14 of the Standard Edition of the Complete Works, London: Hogarth.

Freud, S. (1929), *Introductory Lectures on Psychoanalysis*, London: Allen & Unwin.

Friedman, K. C. (1944), Time concepts of junior and senior high school pupils and of adults, *Sch. R.*, 233–8.

Furth, H. G. (1969), *Piaget and Knowledge*, Englewood Cliffs: Prentice-Hall.

Gagné, R. M. (1970), *The Conditions of Learning* (2nd ed.), New York: Holt, Rinehart & Winston.

Gardner, K. (1969), *Crisis in the Classroom*, Hamlyn.

Gardner, R. W. (1961), Cognitive controls of attention deployment as determinants of visual illusions, *J. Abnorm. Soc. Psychol.*, 62, 120—7.

Gardner, R. W. (1962), Control, defence, and centration effect: a study of scanning behaviour, *Brit. J. Psychol.*, 53, 129—40.

Gardner, R. W. and Long, R. (1962), Control, defence, and centration effect: *Brit. J. Psychol.*, 53, 129—40.

Gardner, R. W. *et al.* (1959), *Cognitive Control*, Psychol. Issues, 4, New York: Int. Univ. Press.

Geach, P. T. (1957), *Mental Acts*, London: Routledge & Kegan Paul.

Gelman, R. (1969), Conservation acquisition: a problem of learning to attend to relevant attributes, *J. Exp. Child Psychol.*, 7, 167—87.

Getzels, J. W. and Jackson, P. W. (1962), *Creativity and Intelligence: Explorations with Gifted Students*, New York: Wiley.

Gill, M. M. (1967), The Primary process, in R. R. Holt, *Psychological Issues: Motives and Thought*, New York: Int. Univ. Press, pp. 260—98.

Goldman, R. J. (1964), *Religious Thinking from Childhood to Adolescence*. London: Routledge and Kegan Paul.

Goldstein, K. and Scheerer, M. (1941), Abstract and concrete behaviour, an experimental study with special tests, *Psychol. Monogr.*, 53, no. 2.

Gollin, E. L. (1954), Forming impressions of personality, *J. Pers.*, 23, 65—76.

Gollin, E. L. (1958), Organisational characteristics of social judgement, a developmental investigation, *J. Pers.*, 26, 139—54.

Guilford, J. P. (1967), *The Nature of Human Intelligence*, New York: McGraw-Hill.

Gurwitsch, A. (1964), *The Field of Consciousness*, Pitsburgh: Duquesne Univ.

Haddon, F. A. and Lytton, H. (1968), Teaching approach and the development of divergent thinking abilities in primary schools, *Brit. J. Ed. Psychol.*, 38, 171—80.

Hanfmann, E. and Kasanin, J. (1937), A method for the study of concept formation, *J. Psychol.*, 3, 521—40.

Hargreaves, D. J. and Bolton, N. (1972), Selection and creativity tests for use in research, *Brit. J. Psychol.*, 63, 451—62.

Harlow, H. F. (1959), Learning set and error factor theory: in *Psychology a Study of Science, Vol. 2* (ed. S. Koch), New York: McGraw-Hill.

Harvey, O. J., Hunt, D. E. and Schroder, H. M. (1961), *Conceptual Systems and Personality Organisation*, New York: Wiley.

Hasan, P. and Butcher, H. J. (1966), Creativity and intelligence: a partial replication with Scottish children of Getzels's and Jackson's study, *Brit. J. Psychol.*, 57, 129—53.

Haslam, J. E. (1966), A study of concept formation in children of average intelligence between the ages of six and sixteen, using Vigotsky's Method, DCP dissertation, Birmingham Univ.

Haygood, R. C. and Bourne, L. E. (1965), Attribute and rule-learning aspects of conceptual behaviour, *Psychol. Rev.*, 72, 175—95.

Heidbreder, E. (1946), The attainment of concepts I, Terminology and methodology, *J. Gen. Psychol.*, 35, 173—189.

Heidbreder, E. (1948), The attainment of concepts IV, Exploratory experiments on conceptualization at perceptual levels, *J. Psychol.*, **26**, 193—216.

Heidbreder, E. (1949), The attainment of concepts VIII, The conceptualization of verbally indicated instances, *J. Psychol.*, **27**, 263—309.

Hofstaetter, P. R. (1954), The changing composition of "intelligence": a study of the T-technique, *J. Genet. Psychol.*, **85**, 159—64.

Horton, R. and Finnegan, R. (1973), *Modes of Thought*, London: Faber.

Hovland, C. I. (1952), A "communication analysis" of concept learning, *Psychol. Rev.*, **59**, 461—72.

Hovland, C. I. and Weiss, W. I. (1953), Transmission of information concerning concepts through positive and negative instances, *J. Exp. Psychol.*, **45**, 175—82.

Howe, C. J. (1976), The meanings of two-word utterances in the speech of young children, *J. Child Language*, 3, 29—47.

Hudson, L. (1968), *Frames of Mind*, London: Methuen.

Hume, D. (1739), *A Treatise of Human Nature*, Oxford: The Clarendon Press (1896).

Hunt, E. B. (1971), What kind of computer is man? *Cognitive Psychol.*, 2, 57—98.

Hunt, E. B., Marin, J. and Stone, P. J. (1966), *Experiments in Induction*, New York: Academic Press.

Hunt, J. McV. (1961), *Intelligence and Experience*, New York: Ronald Press.

Husserl, E. (1900), *Logische Untersuchungen*, Vol. 1, Halle: Niemeyer.

Husserl, E. (1901), *Logische Untersuchungen*, Vol. 2, Halle: Niemeyer.

Husserl, E. (1929), *Formal and Transcendental Logic*, The Hague: M. Nijhoff (1969).

Inhelder, B. and Piaget, J. (1958), *The Growth of Logical Thinking from Childhood to Adolescence*, London: Routledge & Kegan Paul.

Inhelder, B. and Piaget, J. (1964), *The Early Growth of Logic in the Child*, London: Routledge & Kegan Paul.

Inhelder, B. and Sinclair, H. (1969), Learning cognitive structures, in Mussen *et al.*, *Trends and Issues in Developmental Psychology*, New York: Holt Rinehart & Winston.

Inhelder, B., Sinclair, H. and Bovet, M. (1975), *Learning and the Development of Cognition*. London: Routledge and Kegan Paul.

Jahoda, G. (1963), The development of children's ideas about country and nationality, Part II: National symbols and themes, *Brit. J. Ed. Psychol.*, 33, 143—53.

James, W. (1890), *Principles of Psychology*, Vols. 1 and 2, London: Macmillan (1901).

James, W. (1892), *Textbook of Psychology*, New York: Holt.

Jenkins, J. J. (1966), Meaningfulness and concepts: concepts and meaningfulness, in H. J. Klausmeier and C. W. Harris (eds.), *Analyses of Concept Learning*, New York: Academic Press, pp. 65—79.

Jensen, A. R. (1966), Individual differences in concept learning, in H. J. Klausmeier and C. W. Harris, *Analyses of Concept Learning*, New York: Academic Press, pp. 139—54.

Jensen, A. R. (1969), How much can we boost IQ and scholastic achievement? *Harvard Educational Review*, 39, 1—123.

Johnson, P. J. and White, R. M. (1967), Concept of dimensionality and reversal shift performance in children, *J. Exp. Child Psychol.*, 51, 223—7.

Jones, R. M (1968), *Fantasy and Feeling in Education*, Harmondsworth, England: Penguin.

Kagan, J. (1964), The child's sex-role classification of school objects, *Child Dev.*, 35, 1051−6.

Kagan, J. (1971), *Change and Continuity in Infancy*, New York: Wiley.

Kagan, J. *et al.* (1964), Information processing in the child: significance of analytic and reflective attitudes, *Psychol. Monogr.*, 78 (1, Whole No. 578).

Kasanin, J. S. (1945), Developmental roots of schizophrenia, *Amer. J. Psychiat.*, 101, 770−6.

Kelly, G. A. (1955), *The Psychology of Personal Constructs*, New York: Norton (2 Vols).

Kendler, H. H. and D'Amato, M. F. (1955), A comparison of reversal and non-reversal shifts in human concept formation behaviour, *J. Exp. Psychol.*, 49, 165−74.

Kendler, H. H. and Kendler, T. S. (1962), Vertical and horizontal processes in problem solving, *Psychol. Rev.*, 69, 1−16.

Kohlberg, L. (1971), From Is to Ought, in Mischell (ed.), *Cognitive Development and Epistemology*, New York: Academic Press.

Kris, E. (1953), *Psychoanalytic Explorations in Art*, London: Allen & Unwin.

Levine, M. (1966), Hypothesis behaviour by humans during discrimination learning, *J. Exp. Psychol.*, 71, 331−6.

Livesley, W. J. and Bromley, D. B. (1973), *Person Perception in Childhood and Adolescence*, London: Wiley.

Locke, J. (1690), *Essay on the Human Understanding*, Oxford: Clarendon Press (1924), Abridged Edition.

Luborsky, L., Blinder, B. and Schimek, J. C. (1965), Looking, recalling, and GSR as a function of defense, *J. Abnorm. Psychol.*, 70, 270−80.

Lumsden, E. A. and Poteat, W. S. (1968), The salience of the vertical dimension in the concept of "bigger" in five and six year olds, *J. Verb. Learn. Verb. Behav.*, 7, 404−8.

Lunzer, E. A. (1968), Children's Thinking, in H. J. Butcher (ed.), *Educational Research in Britain*, London: Univ. London Press, pp. 69−100.

Macnamara, J. (1972), Cognitive basis of language learning in infants, *Psychol. Rev.*, 79, 1−13.

Mandelbaum, M. (1965), Family resemblances and generalization concerning the arts, *The American Phil. Quart.*, 2, 519−34.

Manis, M. (1971), *An Introduction to Cognitive Psychology*, Belmont, U.S.A.: Brooks-Cole.

Martorella, P. H. (1971), *Concept Learning in the Social Studies*, Scanton, U.S.A.: Intext Ed. Pub.

Mayo, E. (1945), *The Social Problems of an Industrial Civilization*, Boston: Division of Research, Harvard Univ. Grad. School Business Administration.

McNeill, D. (1970), *The Acquisition of Language*, New York: Harper & Row.

Merleau-Ponty, M. (1962), *The Phenomenology of Perception*, London: Routledge & Kegan Paul.

Mill, J. S. (1874), *A System of Logic*, 6th ed., London: Harper.

Miller, G. A., Galanter, E. and Pribram, K. H. (1960), *Plans and the Structure of Behaviour*, New York: Holt, Rinehart & Winston.

Munsinger, H., Kessen, W. and Kessen, M. L. (1964), Age and uncertainty: developmental variation in preference for variability, *J. Exp. Child Psychol.*, 1, 1−15.

Musil, R. (1953), *The Man Without Qualities*, 3 Vols, London: Secker & Warburg.

Neisser, U. and Weene, P. (1962), Hierarchies in concept attainment, *J. Exp. Psychol.*, 64, 640–5.

Osgood, C. E., Suci, G. and Tannenbaum, P. (1957), *The Measurement of Meaning*, Urbana: Univ. Illinois Press.

Parsons, C. (1960), Inhelder and Piaget's "The Growth of Logical Thinking": 2 – a logician's viewpoint, *Brit. J. Psychol.*, 51, 75–84.

Payne, R. W. (1960), Cognitive Abnormalities, in H. J. Eysenck (ed.), *Handbook of Abnormal Psychology*, 1st ed., London: Pitman, pp. 193–261.

Peters, R. S. (1958), *The Concept of Motivation*, London: Routledge & Kegan Paul.

Piaget, J. (1926), *The Language and Thought of the Child*, New York: Harcourt, Brace.

Piaget, J. (1928), *Judgement and Reasoning in the Child*, New York: Harcourt, Brace.

Piaget, J. (1932), *The Moral Judgment of the Child*, London: Routledge & Kegan Paul.

Piaget, J. (1950), *The Psychology of Intelligence*, London: Routledge & Kegan Paul.

Piaget, J. (1951), *Play, Dreams, and Imitation in Childhood*, New York: Norton.

Piaget, J. (1952), *The Child's Conception of Number*, New York: Humanities.

Piaget, J. (1957), Logique et équilibre dans les comportments du sujet, in L. Apostel, B. Mandelbrot and J. Piaget, *Logique et Equilibre. Études d'épistemologie génétique*, Vol. 2, Paris: Presses Univ. France, pp. 27–117.

Piaget, J. (1968), Quantification, conservation and nativism: quantitative evaluations of children aged two to three years are examined, *Science*, 162, 976–81.

Piaget, J. (1969), *The Mechanisms of Perception*, London: Routledge & Kegan Paul.

Piaget, J. and Inhelder, B. (1971), *Mental Imagery in the Child*, London: Routledge & Kegan Paul.

Piaget, J., Vinh-Bang and Matalon, B. (1958), Note on the law of the temporal maximum of some optico-geometric illusions, *Amer. J. Psychol.*, 71, 277–82.

Pikas, A. (1966), *Abstraction and Concept Formation*, Cambridge, Mass.: Harvard Univ. Press.

Polanyi, M. (1959), *The Study of Man*, London: Routledge & Kegan Paul.

Polanyi, M. (1967), *The Tacit Dimension*, London: Routledge & Kegan Paul.

Razran, G. H. S. (1933), Conditioned responses in children: a behavioural and quantitative review of experimental studies, *Arch. Psychol.*, 23, no. 148, 120.

Restle, F. (1961), Statistical methods for a theory of cue learning, *Psychometrika*, 26, 291–306.

Restle, F. (1962), The selection of strategies in cue learning, *Psychol. Rev.*, 69, 329–43.

Richards, P. N. and Bolton, N. (1971), Divergent thinking, mathematical ability, and type of mathematics teaching in junior school children, *Brit. J. Ed. Psychol.*, 41, 32–7.

Rogers, C. (1965), *Client-centred Therapy*, Boston: Houghton Mifflin.

Rokeach, M. (1951), Prejudice, concreteness of thinking and reification of thinking, *J. Abnorm. Soc. Psychol.*, 46, 83–91.

Rommetveit, R. (1961), Perceptual, behavioural and ideational components of discriminatory and conceptual activities, *Acta Psychol.*, 18, 201–17.

Rommetveit, R. (1965), Stages in concept formation, II, *Scand. J. Psychol.*, 6, 59–64.

Rommetveit, R. and Kvale, S. (1965a), Stages in concept formation, III. *Scand. J. Psychol.*, 6, 65–74.

Rommetveit, R. and Kvale, S. (1965b), Stages in concept formation, IV. _Scand. J. Psychol._, 6, 75–9.

Ryan, J. (1974), Early language development: towards a communicational analysis, in M. P. M. Richards (ed.), _The Integration of a Child into a Social World_, London: Cambridge Univ. Press, pp. 185–213.

Schroth, M. L. and Tamayo, F. M. V. (1972), Disjunctive concept formation under different information conditions, _J. Gen. Psychol._, 86, 273–8.

Schutz, A. (1966), _Collected Papers, Vol. 3_, The Hague: Martinus Nijhoff.

Semeonoff, B. and Trist, E. (1958), _Diagnostic Performance Tests: A Manual for Use With Adults_, London: Tavistock.

Sigel, I. E. and Hooper, F. H. (1968), _Logical Thinking in Children_, New York: Holt, Rinehart & Winston.

Silverman, J. (1964), The problem of attention in research and theory in schizophrenia, _Psychol. Rev._, 71, 359–79.

Sinclair-de-Zwart, M. (1967), _Acquisition de Langage et Development de la Pensée_, Paris: Dunod.

Skemp, R. R. (1963), A three part theory for learning mathematics, in F. W. Land (ed.), _New Approaches to Mathematics Teaching_, London: Macmillan.

Skemp, R. R. (1971), _The Psychology of Learning Mathematics_, Harmondsworth, England: Penguin.

Slamecka, N. J. A. (1968), A methodological analysis of shift paradigms in human discrimination learning, _Psychol. Bull._, 69, 423–38.

Smedslund, J. (1961a), The acquisition of conservation of substance and weight in children. V. Practice in conflict situations without external reinforcement, _Scand. J. Psychol._, 2, 156–60.

Smedslund, J. (1961b), The acquisition of conservation of substance and weight in children. VI. Practice on continuous vs. discontinuous material in problem situations without external reinforcement, _Scand. J. Psychol._, 2, 203–10.

Smedslund, J. (1963), The concept of correlation in adults, _Scand. J. Psychol._, 4, 167–73.

Smoke, K. L. (1933), Negative instances in concept learning, _J. Exp. Psychol._, 16, 583–8.

Spiegelberg, H. (1965), _The Phenomenological Movement_, 2 Vols, The Hague: Martinus Nijhoff (2nd ed.).

Stenild, M. (1972), Stages in concept learning, _Scand. J. Psychol._, 13, 98–108.

Stones, E. and Heslop, J. R. (1968), The formation and extension of class concepts in primary school children, _Brit. J. Psychol._, 38, 261–71.

Stout, G. F. (1902), _Analytic Psychology_, London.

Strauss, S. and Langer, J. (1970), Operational thought inducement, _Child Dev._, 41, 163.

Stroop, J. R. (1935a), The basis of Logon's theory, _Amer. J. Psychol._, 47, 499–504.

Stroop, J. R. (1935b), Studies of interference in serial verbal reaction, _J. Exp. Psychol._, 18, 643–72.

Sturt, M. (1925), _The Psychology of Time_, London: Routledge.

Suppes, P. and Schlag-Rey (1965), Observable changes in hypotheses under positive reinforcement, _Science_, 148, 661–2.

Thomas, A., Chess, S. and Birch, H. G. (1968), _Temperament and Behaviour Disorders in Childhood_, New York: Univ. Press.

Tighe, L. S. (1965), Effect of perceptual pretraining on reversal and nonreversal shifts, _J. Exp. Psychol._, 70, 379–85.

Tighe, T. J. and Tighe, L. S. (1968), Perceptual learning in the discrimination processes of children: an analysis of five variables in perceptual pretraining, *J. Exp. Psychol.*, **77**, 125–34.

Tighe, T. J. and Tighe, L. S. (1969), Facilitation of transposition and reversal learning in children by prior perceptual training, *J. Exp. Child Psychol.*, **8**, 366–74.

Trabasso, T. and Bower, G. (1966), Presolution dimensional shifts in concept identification: a test of the sampling with replacement axiom in all-or-none models, *J. Math. Psychol.*, **3**, 163–73.

Trabasso, T., Rollins, H. and Shaughnessy, E. (1971), Storage and verification stages in processing concepts, *Cognitive Psychol.*, **2**, 239–89.

Van de Geer, J. P. and Jaspars, J. M. F. (1966), Cognitive Functions, in *Annual Review of Psychology*, Palo Alto: Annual Reviews Inc., pp. 145–76.

Venables, P. H. (1964), Input dysfunction in schizophrenia, in B. Maher (ed.), *Progress in Experimental Personality Research*, Vol. 1, New York: Academic Press, pp. 1–49.

Vinacke, W. E. (1952), *The Psychology of Thinking*, New York: McGraw-Hill.

Vygotsky, L. S. (1962), *Thought and Language*, New York: Wiley.

Wachtel, P. (1967), Conceptions of broad and narrow attention, *Psychol. Bull.*, **68**, 417–29.

Wallach, M. A. and Kogan, N. (1965), *Modes of Thinking in Young Children*, New York: Holt, Rinehart & Winston.

Ward, W. C. (1969), Creativity and environmental cues in nursery school children, *Devel. Psychol.*, **1**, 543–7.

Watts, A. F. (1944), *The Language and Mental Development of Children*, London: Harrap.

Wechsler, D. (1958), *The Measurement and Appraisal of Adult Intelligence*, Baltimore: Williams & Wilkins.

Werner, H. (1948), *The Comparative Psychology of Mental Development*, New York: Wiley.

Werner, H. and Kaplan, B. (1963), *Symbol Formation*, New York: Wiley.

Wetherick, N. (1976), Concept learning as propositional input, Paper read at the *Annual Conference of the British Psychological Society*, York, 1976.

White, B. L. (1972), *Human Infants: Experience and Psychological Development*, Englewood Cliffs, New Jersey: Prentice-Hall.

White, R. M. and Johnson, P. J. (1968), Concept of dimensionality and optional shift performance in nursery school children, *J. Exp. Child Psychol.*, **6**, 113–19.

White, S. H. (1965), Evidence for a hierarchical arrangement of learning processes, in L. P. Lipsitt and C. C. Spiker (eds.), *Advances in Child Development and Behaviour*, Vol. 2, New York: Academic Press.

Witkin, H. A. (1965), Psychological differentiation and forms of pathology, *J. Abnorm. Psychol.*, **70**, 317–36.

Witkin, H. A. *et al.* (1962), *Psychological Differentiation*, New York: Wiley.

Wittgenstein, L. (1953), *Philosophical Investigations*, Oxford: Basil Blackwell.

Wolff, J. L. (1967), Concept-shift and discrimination reversal learning in humans, *Psychol. Bull.*, **68**, 369–408.

Woodward, M. (1959), The behaviour of idiots interpreted by Piaget's theory of sensori-motor development, *Brit. J. Ed. Psychol.*, **29**, 60–71.

Youniss, J. (1971), Classificatory schemes in relation to class inclusion before and after training, *Human Dev.*, **14**, 171–83.

Zaslow, R. W. (1950), A new approach to the problem of conceptual thinking in schizophrenia, *J. Cons. Psychol.*, **14**, 335–9.

Name Index

157

Subject Index